Per Mare Per Terram

A History of the Royal Marines

Peter C. Smith

Per Mare Per Terram

A History of the Royal Marines

First Edition 1974

A Balfour Book,
Designed, Printed and Published by
Photo Precision Ltd.,
St. Ives, Huntingdon,
Cambridgeshire, PE17 4LS

ISBN 0 85944 017 6

Contents

Acknowledgements

Author and Publisher would like to thank the Commandant General and all the officers and men of the Royal Marines who helped in the preparation of this book, in particular Major A.J. Donald, Corps Archivist. Others who helped include Major A.G.Brown, M.B.E., Curator of the Royal Marines Museum; Captain D.A. Oakley, Editor of *The Globe & Laurel;* Captain M.E.Heathcote, and Corporal N. Clark, Photographer, Department of the Commandant General, Royal Marines. Thanks are due also to the artist Charles C.Stadden for permission to reproduce some of his original paintings and to Stamp Publicity (Worthing) Limited for use of some commemorative cover material. And to Miss D.E.Williams of the National Maritime Museum, Greenwich, and to Miss M.Allum of the National Army Museum, Chelsea, for help in researching the origins of some of the illustrations. Also to Captain R.G. Hollies-Smith F.R.G.S. of the Parker Gallery, London; to Lieutenant-Colonel C.E.J. Eagles, R.M., for permission to reproduce some coloured plates by V. Huen and C. Field from Colonel C. Field's *Britain's Sea Soldiers* and to F.W. Greenacre, Curator of the Department of Fine Art, City Art Gallery, Bristol, for permission to reproduce one of their paintings.

Foreword

Admiral of the Fleet
The Earl Mountbatten of Burma,
K.G., P.C., G.C.B., O.M., G.C.S.I., G.C.I.E.,
G.C.V.O., D.S.O.
Life Colonel Commandant, Royal Marines.

I am proud to write the Foreword to this history, which portrays some of the gallant and exciting exploits of the Royal Navy's seagoing soldiers, the Royal Marines.

My family, including Prince Philip, our Captain General, have had a special interest in the Royal Marines for 270 years, ever since an ancestor of ours, Prince George of Hesse-Darmstadt, personally led and commanded 1,900 Marines in their assault and capture of Gibraltar in 1704.

In 1882 my father landed at Alexandria in command of the Naval Gatling Gun Battery from H.M.S. *Inconstant* with a mixed force of Seamen and Marines.

I inherited his high regard and affection for 'Her Majesty's Jollies', as the Royal Marines are nicknamed. In my first ship, Admiral Beatty's Flagship, H.M.S. *Lion*, Major F.J.W. Harvey won the V.C. in command of the Marines 13.5 inch 'Q' turret at the Battle of Jutland.

I received my first instruction in Wireless Telegraphy from Royal Marines instructors in 1916 as a Midshipman in the *Lion* from Lieutenant Harold Franks and in 1917 in the *Queen Elizabeth* from Major Bernard Gardiner. This gave me my first interest in communications in which I subsequently specialized.

As Chief of Combined Operations in 1942/43 I was responsible for getting Royal Marines to man amphibious craft and subsequently when the Royal Marines Division came under my command I converted them from Infantry to Commandos. They covered themselves with glory and have retained this role ever since.

In this, and my next appointment as Supreme Allied Commander, South East Asia, I was fortunate in having outstanding Royal Marines Officers to fill important positions on my staff.

I know of no finer bands, particularly massed bands, than those of the Royal Marines. The music of the March of the Preobrajensky Guards was presented by their Colonel-in-Chief, my uncle Czar Nicholas II, to my cousin, King Alfonso XIII of Spain, for his Halberdier Guards. He passed the music to me for any Royal Marines Bands under my command and at their Tercentenary in 1964 I gave it to the Corps. They adopted the Preobrajensky March as their Regimental Slow March.

In 1965, on retirement as Chief of the Defence Staff, the Corps did me the great honour of appointing me as their Life Colonel Commandant, which really thrilled me.

Of course this is not the first account of such a historic corps, but the author, Peter Smith, has produced a fascinating history with many fine pictures reproduced for the first time and I hope it will have a well earned success.

Mountbatten of Burma

Opposite:
Royal Marine Artillery Sabretache for mounted officers, 1872-1901. (R. M. Museum).

The original uniform of an officer of the Admiral's Regiment. *(From the painting by Lieutenant Colonel H.A. Bass, R.M., R.M.B. Stonehouse).*

The Admiral's Regiment

Whereas it had long been the custom for certain regiments to embark and fight from time to time in the ships of the Royal Navy it was not until the refinement of the military and the naval arts of warfare, fully developed under Cromwell and his 'Generals at Sea', that the need for a specially trained and equipped force to accompany the fleet became apparent. In the expeditions to the West Indies during the Commonwealth's dispute with Spain success or failure tended to depend on the skill and correct use of the troops embarked, and the fall of Jamaica was an instance that could be cited in justification of such a force.

However, it was not until some years after the Restoration, at the time of the outbreak of the Second Dutch War in 1664, that an Order in Council, issued on October 28th of that year, called for the establishment of a regiment of 1,200 men, to be armed with firelocks, the first such mass issue of this weapon. Termed 'Land souldjers' their duties were in fact spelt out in accordance with 'A Report From the Lords the Committee for the Affayres of his Mats. Navy Royall and Admiralty'.

These troops were to be raised in the City of London, and many of the recruits came from the Trained Bands of the City. From this ancient association has come down the right of the Royal Marines to march through the City with, 'drums beating, colours flying and bayonets fixed'. The name of the regiment was The Duke of York and Albany's Maritime Regiment of Foot, as it was raised by command of the Lord Admiral, later to become King James II, and it was also known as the Lord Admiral's or Admiral's Regiment.

It was gorgeously arrayed in yellow coats, red breeches and stockings, with hats bound with gold braid. The choice of colours is open to question, some stating that it was merely the Duke of York's favourite colour but Colonel C. Field goes deeper than this and asserts that this came from Cromwell's special companies of 'Firelocks' which were dressed in 'Tawney Yellow' rather than red. The Regiment took the precedence of third of the. line and was first commanded by Colonel Sir William Killigrew.

The Regiment served afloat throughout the major battles of the war, being present at the sea fights off Lowestoft in 1665 and the Four Days Battle, the Battle of St. James' Day and 'Holmes Bonfire', the burning of the Dutch Fleet, all in 1666. The tables were turned in the spring of 1667 when the English were caught with their fleet largely still laid up in winter quarters and their crews unpaid and unready. De Ruyter destroyed shipping at Sheerness and penetrated boldly into the Medway. He also landed troops at Harwich, which gave the Admiral's Regiment its first major taste of action ashore.

Such an attack had been foreseen and several companies of the Admiral's Regiment had been concentrated, six in Harwich itself and two

Silver models depicting officers and men of the Admiral's Regiment. *(R.M.B. Stonehouse).*

more, under Captains Darrell and Cartwright, in the Landguard Fort which commanded the harbour entrance. The entrance itself was readied for blocking and so when, on July 2nd, the Dutch Fleet appeared, all was ready to give them a fierce reception. De Ruyter with 47 warships landed an army of 3,000 men under the cliffs at Filstow, out of range of the fort, and then made two determined attacks upon it. The *London Gazette* gave this description:

> 'Near 2,000 of them marched up and made two assaults upon Landguard Fort, where they were stoutly entertained, and after three-quarters of an hour's dispute in the first assault, and about a quarter of an hour's only in the second, they were forced to retire in such haste, that they left their ladders all behind them, scarcely being able to carry off their dead which is judged to be about 150 at the least'.

In the subsequent Third Dutch War the Admiral's Regiment again saw much employment, in Holland itself with the French army and again at Strasburg. In 1676 a detachment went to Virginia. Included in their ranks at this time was one Captain John Churchill, newly promoted from the First Guards, who also fought at sea. Both he and his two brothers served with the Admiral's Regiment, John going on to become famous as that great soldier the Duke of Marlborough. Britain dropped out of the conflict in 1674 and in 1680 the regiment served at Tangier which then was British. A decisive defeat was inflicted on the Moors in October of that year.

The Prince of Denmark's Regiment

When, in 1685, the then Duke of York became King James II the Admiral's Regiment was renamed although remaining, in essence, the same military unit. It was always the custom in those days to name regiments by the names of their commanding officers and thus the Maritime regiment was taken over by Prince George. He was the hereditary Prince of Denmark and the regiment was accordingly so named. It did not take part in any great action under this title, and indeed only existed for a mere four years in this guise.

One thing the change of title did bring with it of more lasting effect was the change in dress and uniform. Apparently Prince George did not share his predecessor's affection for the colour yellow. It was therefore directed that his regiment be clad in what was to become the traditional British red coat, with yellow facings and with it they wore dark grey breeches and white stockings.

In 1688 the regiment was to be dispersed along the south-east coast in order to forestall the expected landing of William of Orange to claim the English throne from James. William in fact landed further to the west, at Torbay, and on his long march towards London many of the defending forces went over to his cause. Poor King James was much distressed but there was no staying the trend. The Marine Regiment was allegedly instructed by William to take itself to Huntingdon, out of the way, and this it apparently did without much opposition, but their previous record of loyalty to the throne of the Stuarts did not commend them to the new King and Queen. Accordingly, in 1689, William and Mary ordered the disbandment of the Prince's Regiment and its men were taken into the Coldstream Guards, while Prince George himself was given command of the Holland regiment (The Buffs) which adopted his name for a time. But the nation remained without a Maritime regiment for only a very short period for England was soon at war again and once more the need for expert 'Sea Soldiers' became paramount.

The uniform of the Prince of Denmark's Regiment. (From the painting by V. Heun in *Britain's Sea Soldiers* by Colonel C. Field).

Torrington's and Pembroke's Marines

It was in 1690 that orders were given for the re-formation of the Marines, but this time it was not from the Royal Family that they took their titles. Two regiments were raised, each to consist of fifteen companies and each company to be two hundred men strong. The first of these large commands was entrusted to the Earl of Torrington. He had seen hard service afloat and was a particularly apt choice. It was he who had been appointed commander of the fleet which brought William to England. The other regiment was to be commanded by the Earl of Pembroke, who was in service at the Admiralty. There were remnants only, among the ranks of these new Marines regiments, of those that had served earlier and it is recorded that only a single officer, one Gilbert Simon, had originally served in the old Marines regiment.

Their uniforms apparently remained the now well-established red but this time with green facings, although Colonel Field's study suggests that an alternative, and appropriate, choice of colour came under consideration but was never utilised. That was blue, lined with white and topped by Grenadier caps. As before, the Marines were to be armed exclusively as fusiliers.

Both regiments were at full strength for the siege of Cork and the fleet had earlier had a good complement aboard when it engaged the French at the Battle of Beachy Head the preceding June. In this first sea battle the Corps suffered very heavy losses by some accounts and at Cork that October they were again in the forefront. In September these Marines were with the Faringdon expedition to Jamaica. Heavy losses over the years reduced their ranks so that in July, 1698, they were amalgamated under Colonel Thomas Brudenall, while their places in line were filled by three infantry regiments of reduced strength. But with the ending of the war in October, 1697, and the chaotic state of the Admiralty finances there came a disbandment once more, in May, 1699, with scant ceremony.

Gibraltar; Capture and Defence

It had long been British policy on the Continent to prevent any one European power from dominating it and with the death of the Spanish monarch, Carlos II, in November, 1701, this policy was again under pressure. Louis XIV of France, already the most powerful ruler of his day, laid claim to the throne for his grandson, Philip. Such a move the British and Dutch were not prepared to contemplate, and the War of the Spanish Succession followed. Already, when it was likely that such a conflict would develop, the Marines had been reconstituted, Queen Anne ordering, on 1st

June, the formation of no less than six regiments of Marines, and six other regiments for 'Sea Service'. Colonel Seymour was appointed Superintendent of the Marine Regiments, with Prince George remaining as Lord High Admiral. These new regiments contained a high proportion of officers and, most likely, men also from the four recently disbanded regiments, thus retaining a strong continuity.

Elements from these regiments were to see action in 1702 at the abortive attempt to storm Cadiz and in the subsequent, better-favoured, attack on the Spanish treasure fleet at Vigo. Portugal joined the Grand Alliance of England, France and Austria in 1704, and a large Anglo-Dutch force went to Lisbon, and subsequently dallied outside Barcelona and Cadiz. Admiral Rooke was hesitant at again attacking the latter after the previous failure but was more agreeable when Prince George put forward the alternative target of Gibraltar. Accordingly on 21st July, 1704, the Prince of Hesse led ashore 1,900 Marines to sever the isthmus and lay siege to the garrison under Don Diego de Salinas. It is of wry interest to note that although the British were fighting to place the Austrian Archduke Charles upon the throne, Admiral Rooke and the British Government were in no doubt about the future of the Rock should it fall, for Gibraltar had long been a coveted fortress to command the approach to the rich Mediterranean.

The Spanish Governor was called upon to surrender but refused and therefore, after some brief skirmishing, Admiral Rooke ordered the fleet to make a determined bombardment of the defence works of the fortress. Lieutenant Paul Nicolas, in his *Historical Record of the Royal Marine Forces*, says:

> 'On 22nd the admiral, at break of day, commenced a vigorous attack and cannonaded the town with so much spirit that fifteen thousand shot were expended in the course of five hours. This produced a correspondent effect, and Sir George Rooke, perceiving that the enemy were driven from the works at the mole ahead, ordered Captain Whitaker to arm all the boats and attempt to make himself master of the enemy's fortifications; justly concluding, that if these were once occupied, the town must immediately surrender. This order was no sooner issued, than Captains Hicks and Jumper, who were nearest to the mole, pushed ashore with their pinnaces; and having scrambled up into the fortifications, were actually in possession of them before the rest of the attacking party could arrive. The Spaniards, finding the works untenable, sprang a mine, by which explosion two lieutenants and forty men were killed, and sixty wounded. Notwithstanding this misfortune, the two captains maintained possession of the great platform until they were

The attack on Gibraltar, 1704. (From the print *Prise de Gibraltar* by N. Ozanne, R.M. Museum).

sustained by Captain Whitaker and the seamen under his command.'

Although the Spanish garrison was described as a small one, only 500 men in all, it had been stated that the defences were strong enough to be manned by fifty men who could have defended the Rock against thousands. On 26th July the Spanish surrendered and the Prince of Hesse hoisted a standard and proclaimed King Charles as ruler of Spain. Admiral Rooke, however, did not consider that good English lives had been expended to hand Gibraltar to Austria. He had the offending flag quickly run down and took possession of Gibraltar in the name of Queen Anne.

In August the indecisive battle of Malaga was fought between the English and French fleets and when it was broken off Rooke had to return for refitting and reinforcement. Before he did so he landed at Gibraltar all his available Marines, sixty guns, and rations for three months. Soon after he had left, the first signs of the returning Spanish armies appeared and, by October 4th, a French fleet arrived with more French and Spanish troops. The long siege began during which the Marines bore the brunt of the fighting, they being the largest contingent on the Rock.

A strong army under The Marquis de Villadarias, a Spanish grandee, soon began assault after assault to take Gibraltar back. Trench work began on October 9th but the Spanish only made slow progress at first and the Marines constantly sortied against the working parties to further delay their work. Constant artillery preparations were made and on

November 10th a determined attack was to have been attempted. This was thwarted by the arrival of a convoy with food and arms brought in by the ships of Sir John Leake's command.

While orthodox siege methods continued to be employed by the Spanish the Marquis de Villadarias had also decided to try to storm the fortress by what was termed 'a forlorn hope' party of some 400 men who scaled the top of the Rock by a footpath on the eastern side, under the command of Colonel Figeura. They succeeded in reaching St. Michael's Cave where they concealed themselves and then at dawn took the Signal Station atop the Rock in a rush. So far they had succeeded beyond their greatest hopes but now the alarm was given and 500 Marines sortied under Colonel Bor to counter-attack them. By some oversight these gallant Spaniards had only been issued with three rounds per man, and the Spanish General also failed to put in his promised diversionary attack. The result was a foregone conclusion, and the little force was cut to pieces with the loss of 200 killed and 190 prisoners.

Although by December the Marines had been reduced by sickness and wounds to around 1,000 men, another convoy got through and the Spanish army was in even worse straits, with a loss of 12,000 men by the end of the campaign, almost all because of disease or desertion. One Spanish source revealed that:

> 'The Council had been very much taken up of late in the finding out funds for continuing the war, especially for carrying on the Siege of Gibraltar, which is a great expense'.

Another major assault was launched on February 2nd, 1705, when some 1,000 men stormed the Round Tower which was defended by less than two hundred Marines. A close and hard-fought combat resulted in heavy losses on both sides. Reinforcements were sent by the French and a further great attack was repulsed from the Land Port at the end of February. The English fleet under Sir John Leake again proved itself invaluable and on 20th March he smashed the French fleet commanded by M. de Pointi in the Bay itself. This was the final straw for the Spanish and French and on April 20th, after a siege of some eight months, they blew up their trenches and retired in defeat.

The Triumphs of Her Majesty's Arms, published in 1707, gave praise to the Marines as follows: 'Encouraged by the example of the Prince of Hesse, the garrison did more than could humanly be expected, and the English Marines gained an immortal glory'.

This they indeed did and today 'Gibraltar' remains the sole battle honour to be displayed on the Colours of the Corps.

Meantime the war dragged on and despite Gibraltar it was not marked by many other such victories for British arms.

The Marines were constantly employed all over the world in the years that followed. Prince George himself was killed in the second phase of an attack on Barcelona while with the Earl of Peterborough, later to become Captain-General of the Marine Forces in Great Britain. Far more striking was the taking of Annapolis Royal by the Marines in 1710. This port in Nova Scotia was serving as a base for French privateers harrying trade to the American colonies and 600 Marines, under Colonel Francis Nicholson, were part of a force sent to capture it. Having called at Boston to replenish, the fleet arrived off Annapolis Royal on 23rd September. A landing was effected two days later and, with the Marines in the van, the fort guarding the harbour was assaulted. The regiments advanced 'with drums beating and colours flying' and then entrenched themselves within 400 yards of the fort. After some not very enthusiastic fighting the French Governor surrendered with all the honours of war, the French marched out and the English marched in. Here they found themselves, when left by the expedition, worse off than the defeated French for the forests were full of hostile Indians who massacred a party of seventy men in ambush.

Although the Duke of Marlborough won four crushing victories in Europe he was dismissed by Queen Anne, the Treaty of Utrecht was concluded in 1713 and the war was brought to an end. And so once more, in 1713, the regiments of Marines were dismissed or taken into the line.

The War of the Austrian Succession

All through the intermittent peace the Marines remained disbanded and the four companies of Invalids retained were the only link in the line for almost thirty years. In October, 1739, this peace was ended with the War of Jenkins' Ear which was brought about by Spanish intervention in the peaceful trading of British ships plying to American waters. This became part of the War of the Austrian Succession, which was a re-run of the preceding war, with England siding with Austria against a Franco-Spanish combination which they felt threatened to dominate Europe.

At the opening of Parliament the King declared that, 'a body of Marines should be raised' and the next month, December, 1739, an Order in Council decreed the raising of six Marine regiments. Most of the officers and men were brought in from existing line regiments but not enough trained troops were on hand to supply the fleet under Admiral Anson which was due to set out for South American waters. Instead he was sent five Invalid companies of 500 pensioners. Many of them deserted at Portsmouth and those that were left sailed off with 240 fresh replacements. By the time Anson returned, four years later, after having

A Marine of 1742, a composite painting of the various uniforms of the time. (From the print in *Cannon's Military Records*, 1830).

circumnavigated the globe, most of the ancient veterans had died.

This voyage was notable in Marine annals for the epic courage and fortitude of four Marines from H.M.S. *Wager*, Corporal Crosslet and Privates Smith, Hobbs and Hertford. A misfortune having overcome a small expedition, there remained insufficient room in the one remaining boat for all. These four Marines volunteered to be left behind on the bleak Patagonian coast so that the others might find safety. Stating simply that they were soldiers, 'and knew how to die', they cheered the others as the boat drew away and called 'God bless the King'. A lonely fate and one that would not have come to the ears of the world had not the boat eventually have come through with one survivor to relate the story of their sacrifice. It was later described by Robert Louis Stevenson in his work, *The English Admirals*.

The six newly formed Marine regiments had assembled on the Isle of Wight, which it was recorded was customary, 'on account of the difficulty of deserting from it'. A grand expedition against Cartagena was prepared, against all advice as to the risk of sending thousands of troops to such a fever-infested spot, under the command of General Wentworth ashore and Admiral Vernon afloat. Leaving England in January, 1741, 9,000 strong, the force arrived at Jamaica having lost 600 through death and with a further 1,500 sick. There it found the American contingent, under Colonel Gooch, equally reduced by illness and in a mutinous state having received no wages, no instructions and no food or ammunition.

Cartagena was reached and the assault against the ring of forts began. Eventually the lagoon was reached after heavy fighting and some of the main forts were silenced with very little effort. But here events started to go seriously awry. Ill feeling between the Naval and Military commanders erupted often. Although the city was within their grasp, their plan was first to take Fort St. Lazar. Wentworth asked for further reinforcements before proceeding and camped what troops he had on the disease-ridden swamps. When the attack eventually took place it was against a fore-warned enemy. Misled by their guide, they stumbled in the darkness into the outlying trenches of the Fort where many were shot down. Some pressed on in the face of grape and round shot and raised a single scaling ladder up which a few struggled to the top but all were killed or wounded and the ladder cast down. The survivors were taken in the rear by the guns of Cartagena itself. Colonel Grant of the 5th Marines was hit and before he died his last words summed up the whole ghastly fiasco: 'The General ought to hang the guides, and the King ought to hang the General'. Covered by the 1st Marines, the few survivors struggled back to their ships and then lay for ten days in the lagoon while fever raged unchecked. Only one in ten of this expedition returned to Jamaica.

The Marines saw further service at this period during the capture of Louisburg, Cape Breton, in 1744/45, the great sea fight off Toulon in 1744 and in the suppression of the '45 Rising, culminating in the battle of Culloden in 1746 which ended the hopes of Prince Charles Edward Stuart. Sea fighting took place off Finisterre and Belle Isle in 1747 and the Corps' final assignment was at the siege of Madras. The war closed in 1748 and the six regiments were then disbanded.

Hannah Snell

The famous 'Female Marine', Hannah Snell, has been the subject of several accounts, each of which can be taken with several grains of salt. There seems, however, little doubt that she did in fact really inlist in the Marines and served her full time. Of the adventures and hardships attributed to her during her time in the service many make good reading even if their authenticity can be considered somewhat doubtful.

By all accounts, Hannah was the daughter of a hosier and dyer in Worcester and was born in 1723, being orphaned seventeen years later. While a child she had shown martial learnings and organised her playmates into 'Young Amazon Snell's Company' to parade around the streets of the town. With the death of her parents she went to live with a married sister in Wapping, all her other sisters having married soldiers and her brothers having enlisted. She married a foreigner, 'Dutch Jim' (!) who deserted her and left her with a child, but with nothing else. Hearing he was at Coventry, she decided to join him there after the death of the infant and, finding no trace of him, determined upon joining the Army.

She was enrolled by a corporal into Captain Miller's Company of General Guise's Regiment and marched from Coventry to Carlisle with them. This was the scene of her initial trial with the services. Confided in by her sergeant about his wicked intentions toward a young girl, Hannah, true to her sex, warned the young lady and the sergeant, thinking that his new recruit had anticipated him, trumped up a charge against young Hannah of 'neglect of duty'. 600 lashes was the punishment given as sentence and Hannah is said to have actually received 500 of them and this, it was said, 'made her desert'!.

She made her way to Portsmouth and on 27th November, 1745, she enlisted a second time, this time into the Marines, joining Colonel Fraser's regiment. Three weeks after joining her detachment aboard the sloop *Swallow*, she sailed to join the fleet of Admiral Boscawen which was standing out for the east. Boscawen's expedition left in November, 1794, to attack French possessions but, on arrival off Mauritius, found the enemy too alert for him to attempt to land. The Admiral therefore pressed on to India, arriving at Fort St. David where he was joined by additions under Admiral Griffin and the East India Company. With a force of 5,220 men, including the 880 Marines of the fleet, he determined upon an expedition against the French-held town of Pondicherry. Two attacks against the outlying fortress of Arian Coupan resulted in its capture and seige was then laid to Pondicherry itself. Hannah, it was said, by 'her intrepid conduct acquired the commendation of all the officers'.

In the advance upon Pondicherry, Hannah 'was the first in the party of English foot who forded the river, breast-high, under an incessant fire from a French battery'. During the siege the British forces suffered severely, in miserable conditions, without making much progress. Hannah took her spells at guard duty without flinching and was further recorded as having, 'laboured very hard about fourteen days at throwing up trenches'. Nor was the gallant lady Marine backward when it came to hotter action for in one attack she stood knee-high in the water-filled trench and fired 37 rounds from her musket. In return she was hit twelve times, six bullets entering her right leg and five in her left, while the last inflicted, 'a dangerous flesh wound which, had she applied for assistance, would have revealed her secret'. Hannah had her obvious wounds attended to by the surgeons but she dressed the other wound herself, after removing the bullet with finger and thumb.

She then served aboard the *Eltham* and while at Bombay she was unjustly accused of theft by Lieutenant Wyegate who sentenced her to twelve lashes. Her innocence was subsequently established and Lieutenant Wyegate was 'struck from aloft' by a block and died soon after. She was frequently ashore with her comrades and by joining in wholeheartedly with their exploits kept her true identity a secret, even though on occasions she was, as one history records, 'almost shocked' by their actions.

Hannah finally took her discharge at London and revealed herself during a final drinking session to her astonished shipmates. After a short time as an actress she set up as a publican, opening 'The Widow in Masquerade' at Wapping.

The Grand Divisions

As we have seen, the various Marine Regiments that were raised during the 84 years up to the Peace of Aix-la-Chapelle had been disbanded at the end of each conflict. After his very unhappy experiences with the 'Invalids' which had acompanied his around the world, Admiral Anson was in the forefront of a campaign to make the Marines a permanent organisation. What was needed was a body of men fully trained in all aspects of fighting, ashore and afloat, paid on time and led by officers who saw the Marines as a useful arm with a future. After the debacle at Cartagena the morale of the Corps had suffered considerably and it was felt that it was attributable to poor training and to poor leadership by men indifferent to the Marines traditions.

The Royal Navy had been engaged with the enemy on a world-wide scale rather than restricting themselves to operations only in the North Sea and the Channel and with the growth of colonies far across the globe the need for a steady band of soldiers to accompany the fleets on their distant sorties was also obvious. Therefore after several years of vigorous pushing for such a regular force of Marines, Anson and others were rewarded when, in 1755, with Britain again drifting into war with France and Spain, the Order in Council of 5th April called for the formation of fifty companies of Marines to serve under the Admiralty. These 5,000 regulars were to be formed into three divisions, the 'Grand Divisions' as they later became known, based at the great naval centres of Portsmouth, Chatham and Plymouth. In the same year was passed an Act of Parliament establishing these divisions as permanent bodies, and for almost two centuries these 'divisions' remained the only permanent unit of the Marine Corps.

The 5,000 were raised by the re-enlistment of about half of those men who had been discharged in 1748, with further additions from the line regiments and veterans, but a large proportion still had to be raised in the traditional manner by recruiting parties scouring the countryside and offering bounty. By 1756 the skirmishes in the Americas between France and England had developed into full-scale war and there was little time to fully train the men thus taken. As always Britain suffered reverses on the commencement of hostilities, the most serious being the loss of Minorca, for which the unfortunate Admiral Byng was made the scapegoat of the neglect of the pre-war years, and the rebuff received at the attack on Rochefort in 1757 which was a shambles from start to finish. Such reverses led to the rise of Pitt the elder to power and under his leadership some sharp re-organisation was put into effect. Further attacks were made on the French coast, at Louisberg, Senegal and Goree, which resulted in some successes.

The original plan of the old Stonehouse barracks built at Plymouth in 1783. *(R.M.B. Stonehouse).*

Stonehouse Barracks today, still well preserved in its original form. *(R.M.B. Stonehouse).*

Belle Isle

After the early disappointments of the Seven Years War, 1759 brought a complete change of fortune and became known as the 'Glorious Year of Heart of Oak'. The Army won an important victory at Minden, while the Fleet and the Marines crushed the seapower of France in a series of resounding actions. Boscawen trounced the French off Lagos, Admiral Hawke annihilated another fleet in what they thought were the safe shallows off Quiberon Bay. Admiral Rodney bombarded Le Havre and the Marines were present with General Wolfe at Quebec and were also at the conquest of Guadeloupe. It was however at the conquest of the first piece of French territory to be captured in the war, Belle Isle in 1761, that the Marine Corps won the greatest acclaim and for which, it is believed, they were awarded the laurel wreath.

The island lies off the south-east coast of Brittany and is about fifteen miles long. At its widest point, in the west, it is about twelve miles across, and at its narrowest, in the east, five miles. The largest town and principal harbour is the port of Palais on the eastern side of the northern outjutting 'head' of the island. A previous plan to take the island had been made in 1760 and had been abandoned but the French had reinforced the garrison when the assault was made in April, 1761. The position of this small island, midway between Brest and Bordeaux, was of great importance, and its loss would, it was hoped, pull back French troops from their battles with our Prussian allies.

27

In addition to eleven line regiments and a few artillery pieces, the landing force included a Marine battalion of 800 men, which the Marines of the fleet increased to a total of around 1,400 officers and men. The covering fleet of ten ships of the line, several frigates and four bomb ketches arrived with the convoy off Palais on 7th April. The fleet was under the command of Admiral Keppel and the landing army was under General Hodgson. The first attempt was made to put troops ashore on the 8th, during a diversionary bombardment of the Palais citadel by the fleet. However the French troops were fully alerted and the whole coast had been well prepared, under Governor de St. Croix, to resist invasion. Thus a landing which went in against the fortified positions at Port Andro, on the extreme eastern peninsula, was repulsed after getting ashore, with the loss of over 400 men, while a second attack at Sauzon, on the north-west tip of the island, never even got ashore. Bad weather then blew up and for several days the expedition was beset by storms which threatened to wreck all their landing craft, 'flats' as they were called then. On the 22nd April, however, all was ready for another attempt, and, to the amazement of the French, the second landing was close by where the first had been repulsed. This was the last spot expected and because of this Brigadier Lambert's troops, which included a detachment of Marines, got ashore unopposed. The French defence works were described as being three deep at this spot, with the outer breastwork eighteen feet thick and topped with pallisades made of iron spikes. Once ashore the Marines, under cover of fog, scaled the rocks and cliffs, which the French thought were unapproachable, and formed up with a company of the 19th Foot. They repulsed all French attacks until reinforced by Marines under Lieutenant-Colonel Mackenzie; then, under covering fire from the fleet, they stormed and captured the French positions. Mackenzie and Captain Murray were the only Marines officers who were wounded. An eyewitness account of this splendid achievement was provided by Major Collins of the Marines:

'I had fourteen of my men killed and wounded; and I myself was the first Marine ashore, for which I am made a Major, and at present command 800 men, and have the pleasure to hear everybody speak of the Marines as heroes. I think we shall soon take the town with great ease; as now the landing is made good we think ourselves out of all danger, and as soon as we get our great guns on shore it will be completed'.

That night the French lit a huge beacon as a mute plea for help from the mainland, but although Belle Isle was as close to France as the Isle of Wight is to Portsmouth, the powerful French army was helpless to aid its comrades due to British command of the sea and thus had to stand idly by while the Marines and the Army moved in upon Palais itself.

The Marines acquired a great reputation in this campaign, not least from the enemy. At this period the Marines wore the scarlet uniforms of a line regiment with white facings and on their heads wore the sugar-loaf-shaped caps covered with white cloth. These Marines were rather smaller than the Grenadiers, the sturdiest of the line troops, picked for their height and bearing. When asked which British Troops they most feared, the French reply was, 'les petits grenadiers', the Marines.

It is of interest to note the use of the Marines, so accustomed to the sea and boat-handling work, as the first ashore in this landing. Prior to this attack it was each regiment's grenadiers and light infantry, the flank companies, which were assigned the most dangerous tasks, which had always had this duty. Some delay in the investing of Palais enabled the French to improve their defences and by the time the siege artillery was ashore and in position with trenches dug, the French town was a tougher nut to crack than the gallant Major Collins had earlier envisaged. With reinforcements landed from the warships the Marines were formed into three companies totalling 1,088 men while a further 346 were in detach-

The landings at Belle Isle. This shows the main attack of 22nd April, 1761. (From the black & white print by Serres, National Maritime Museum, Greenwich).

ments in the outposts. A long siege followed, punctuated by desperate sorties by the French garrison, like that of the 3rd May, which was repulsed with great devotion by Marines under Captain David Hepburn at the points of their bayonets.

On the 13th May, 1761, the Marines led the storming of the redoubts with great dash and courage and carried them all, chasing the defenders into the town and up to the walls of the citadel itself across the creek. An account of this remarkable action, against defences that were expected to hold out against determined attacks for weeks, was given thus: —

> 'A furious attack was made upon the enemy's lines which covered the town, and they were carried without much loss, principally by the uncommon intrepidity of a Corps of Marines, which had been but newly raised. No action of greater spirit and gallantry had been performed during the whole war'.

The citadel held out for longer but it too finally surrendered on 7th June and Belle Isle remained British until the war ended in the Peace of Paris in 1763.

The War of American Independence

With the French threat to their existence removed by force of British arms during the Seven Years War, the colonists in North America became more and more restive. The Stamp Act of 1765, passed to provide for their continued military protection, was repealed a year later but, despite this, agitation arose over taxation in this manner from London, even though the colonists were the beneficiaries. This running sore continued to fester until, by the spring of 1775, it was ready to break into all-out rebellion. In anticipation of this, and with a view to damping down the flames of revolt, two Marine battalions were sent to Boston to reinforce the garrison. These Marines were to be directly involved in the first two tragic events which commenced this useless war.

General Gage, the commander of the British troops, received word in April that the rebel American Militia were gathering stores of arms and ammunition, in readiness for an uprising, at Concord, some twenty miles from Boston. He despatched a provisional battalion of some 800 men under Lieutenant-Colonel Smith of the 10th Regiment to confiscate these weapons and nip the rebellion in the bud. With this force went Major Pitcairn of the Marines. However Boston was full of spies and the plan, thought of as a close secret, was in fact betrayed and Paul Revere rode through the countryside warning the rebels. Caught once, he was released in the rather too easy-going manner in which Britain sometimes conducts military affairs, and continued his work. Thus it was that by the time

1755	1760	1775	1773	1789	1795	1805
The Marine Corps	The Marine Corps	The Marine Corps	The Marine Corps	The Marine Corps	The Marine Corps	Royal Marines
(Sergeant)	(Officer with Regt. Colour)	(Grenadier Full Dress)	(Regimental Surgeon)	(Grenadier Marching Order)	(Officer Full Dress)	(Sergeant Full Dress)

1758	1773	1780	1775	1790	1798	1807
The Marine Corps	The Marine Corps	The Marine Corps	The Marine Corps	The Marine Corps	The Marine Corps	Royal Marines
(Drummer)	(Officer Grenadier Coy.)	(Sergeant Grenadier Coy.)	(Private Light Coy.)	(Sergeant Battalion Coy.)	(Officer in Greatcoat)	(Drummer Full Dress)

Uniforms of the Marines from 1755-1807. (From the painting by Charles Stadden, R.M. Museum).

Smith reached Lexington Major Pitcairn, with the advance guard, was ambushed and heavily fired upon. The rebel force was nonetheless dispersed and the guns at Concord broken, but, during their subsequent withdrawal to Boston, the British troops were continually sniped at from behind cover and suffered many casualties.

The situation further worsened in the month that followed and another 600 Marines arrived to reinforce the garrison. The Marine force was divided into two battalions, each consisting of a Grenadier company, a Light Infantry Company and eight Battalion Companies. Boston was blockaded all around on the landward side and, on the prominent heights across the water above the suburb of Charlestown, the American army began digging in, throwing up a formidable redoubt and mounting captured cannon therein. On June 17th, 1775, things came to a head when a signal from the *Lively* revealed these developements to the British commander. Although the rebel position on the neck of land opposite Boston was surrounded on three sides by water and the British could have easily taken it from behind with little trouble, General Gage determined upon a frontal show of strength, some say in the hope of overaweing the Americans and thus saving life, but in the event it was the troops of his own command who were to suffer from his well meant intentions.

General Howe, his second in command, landed some 2,000 troops below the slopes of the citadel atop Bunker Hill and deployed them for a steady advance against the estimated 6,000 rebels entrenched above them. Meanwhile sniping fire from the houses of Charlestown resulted in it being put to the torch. It was a hot day as the scarlet-coated British troops, including the 1st Marine Battalion, readied themselves for the assault.

The Battle of Bunker Hill, 1775. (From the print by
Simkin, National Army Museum, Chelsea).

Lieutenant J. Waller, the Battalion Adjutant, who was present at the
battle describes the events of the next hour in a letter written the day
after:

> 'We landed close under Charles Town, and formed with the 47th
> Regiment close under the natural defences of the redoubt which
> we drove the enemy from, climbing over the rails and hedges.
> So we closed upon them, but when we came immediately under
> the work, we were checked by the severe fire of the enemy, but
> did not retreat an inch.'

The first attack was in fact repulsed as the British, advancing in close
order, were fired upon from trenches and from their flanks. In particular
the Americans concentrated their fire upon the officers who received
casualties out of all proportion to the numbers employed. Another writer
wrote that in the second attack:

> 'The heat was intense what with the sun and the burning town
> of Charles Town close to our left flank. The knapsacks, there-
> fore, were left at the foot of the slope, and some of the men even
> took off their coats. On the left a battalion reduced to a handful
> led the way, followed by the Marines, with the 47th in the rear'.

This time there was no retreat and the British reached the crest of the
hill under withering fire.

> 'The Marines, with the 47th on their left dashed forward with
> a cheer, and were the first over the parapet. The Americans
> gave way along the line and fell back, but their last volley

mortally wounded that gallant old warrior Pitcairn, as, sword in hand, he was cheering on his men. He fell back in the arms of his son, an officer in the 1st Battalion.'

Although, as a result of this, the rebels fled in disorder with heavy losses, the British had casualties of over 1,000 dead and wounded. The siege continued and eventually the British were forced to evacuate Boston taking with them all the Loyalists. Although the war continued it was complicated by the entry of France against Britain in 1778, then Spain in 1779 and finally Holland in 1780. More preoccupied with defending themselves against these three powerful nations than subduing the colonies, the British were finally forced to abandon the area and America received her Independence. France also regained some of her West Indian territories and Britain lost Minorca. The Marines were engaged in minor operations elsewhere and Gibraltar was almost lost, although Negapatam and Trincomalee were taken. The war ended with the Treaty of Versailles in 1783.

The Commonwealth of Australia

Some compensation for the loss of the American Colonies came from the settlement of Australia. The Marines had been among the first to investigate these new lands in the Pacific for they had accompanied Captain Cook on his voyages of exploration during the 1770's. Small groups of Marines had been present at all his landings and were present at his death. This took place on 14th February, 1779, when a misunderstanding over the theft of a boat by the natives led to Cook landing and demanding its return. He was attacked by some of the natives whereupon six Marines of his guard, led by Lieutenant Phillips, gave warning. Cook shot one of his attackers and the men left in the boats opened fire. While trying to get them to cease firing Captain Cook was stabbed in the back by one of the native chiefs, who was, in turn, slain by Lieutenant Phillips.

The despatch of Marines to Australia had been put before the British Government as early as 1773 when it was suggested that two companies of Marines and a score of artificers be sent out as an advance guard to prepare the way for the colonists. This scheme was ignored but in 1786, Lord Sydney, Secretary for the Colonies, authorised settlement of a penal colony at Botany Bay, New South Wales. The Captain of the convoy and designate Governor was Captain A. Phillip, R.N., and as his deputy Major R. Ross of the Marines was appointed. In all some 21 officers and 192 men of the Marine Corps volunteered for the three-year period together with forty of their wives. On 26th January, 1788, Captain Phillip assembled his officers around the flagstaff on the landing site and there they drank toasts to the Royal Family and 'success to the New Colony' and the Marine detachment fired a ceremonial volley of shots into the air. On the 7th February the formal Proclamation of the Colony was read out, the Marines marching behind their band with colours flying to what is now Dawe's Point, while Captain David Collins of the Marines, the Judge Advocate, read out the official declarations.

On 15th February, 1788, Marines were among a number sent to colonise Norfolk Island. Unfortunately Ross did not get on with Phillip and, when his wishes to form a Colonial Corps were turned down, returned to England with almost all his men. However in the ensuing years a second fleet arrived. Collins had meantime established a settlement at the present site of Hobart, in Tasmania.

The first citizen of the state of Victoria was born the son of a Royal Marine, being named on 25th November, 1803, William James Hobart

The founding of the Commonwealth of Australia in 1788.
(From the print by Algernon Talmage, R.M. Museum).

Thorne. In February, 1813, another Governor of the Colony was a Marine, Colonel Thomas Davey.

During the subsequent opening up of the southern Pacific the Marines were again among the pioneers, although the early settlements established at Melville Island in 1824 and at Port Essington in 1837 did not survive for more than a decade. However Australia had not seen the last of the Marines for in December, 1854, the Marines of the *Electra* were involved in crushing the Eureka Stockade rebellion at Ballarat. When New Guinea was annexed in November, 1884, a company of the R.M.L.I. and R.M.A. under Major T.W. Dowding, R.M.L.I. and Lieutenant Drake, R.M.A. paraded as a Guard of Honour at Port Moresby.

The Revolutionary War

The Revolutionary Government in France considered itself merely the forerunner of a world-wide system and declared that all monarchy and established forms of government were its enemies. War was declared on Britain in 1793, and this country, which had watched the barbarism across the water with some distaste, immediately set about forming a coalition with other governments against the French who had brutally invaded the Netherlands.

As had happened so often before, the Navy and the Marine Corps had been run down to a perilous state and so short was the country of the latter that line regiments had once more to be sent to sea until the deficiency could be made up. In the opening moves of the new conflict, an expeditionary force was despatched to help the Netherlands and another was sent to Toulon as a diversion. Lord Hood led a British squadron into the port to join with French loyalists and among the 1,500 troops landed was a company of Marines under Captain Richard Bidlake who occupied Fort la Malgue on August 18th, 1793.

A large Republican army soon arrived to retake the town and heavy and bitter fighting continued until December. One episode can be related from the many actions during this time. A small redoubt was held in the defence line by 120 Marines under Lieutenant Thomas Naylor. They were attacked suddenly by a column of 2,000 Republicans through a fog. However the redoubt was ready for them, and Naylor allowed the French to come within close range before opening fire. A quarter of the attackers melted away before this steady defence before the rest fled. But eventually the town had to be evacuated, the loyal French being taken off with the British troops to prevent their massacre. It was during this siege that Napoleon Bonaparte first encountered the Marines, who, one story says, he had wished to join at one stage of his youth.

French possessions in the West Indies were attacked by British fleets, and Martinique, St. Lucia and Trinidad were all taken. At Martinique on February 5th, 1793, Captain Thomas Oldfield led the Marines into the trenches at the St. Nicholas Mole and struck the enemy colours. Some 320 Marines were present when St. Lucia was taken on 27th April, 1796, and their action was reported as follows: 'The Conduct of the marines upon this, as upon all other occasions, were perfectly correct'.

At sea, the Marines were present at the victory of the 'Glorious First of June' in 1794 when Lord Howe completely defeated a French force of equal size. The Marines were serving in thirteen ships of the fleet during this action. When the *Marlborough* had all her colours shot away she was fired upon in error by several British ships until a seaman stripped the red coat from a dead Marine and hoisted it aloft in their place.

The French having subjugated the Netherlands, the British reacted by seizing the Cape of Good Hope. In the campaign, fought between August and November, 1795, some 350 Marines under Major Hill took part. They fought at Muizenburg and were commended by the Army commander, 'for their steadiness and resolution'.

In 1797 came another great victory at sea when Sir John Jervis with fifteen ships of the line smashed a Spanish fleet of twenty-seven vessels off Cape St. Vincent on the 14th August. The following year was fought the Battle of Camperdown, when the Dutch were defeated by a British squadron on 11th October. In 1797, with Napoleon establishing an army in Egypt, his fleet was again smashed by the brilliance of Nelson at the Battle of the Nile, on 1st August. Aboard the *Orion*, before the battle, Sir James Saumarez stirred his crew to a fighting pitch with a long speech appealing to their duty to King and Country, their wives and families and the like. On the conclusion of his lengthy oration he requested Captain John Savage of the Marines to address his men in similar fashion. Savage turned to his men and asked them, "Do you see these ships, and do you see that land there?". When they shouted "Aye", Savage went on, "Well, those are the enemy's ships, and that's the land of Egypt, and if you don't give those Frenchmen a damned good licking, you'll soon be in the House of Bondage!". His speech was equally as effective as the Admiral's!

Typical of the many smaller actions was that which took place on 7th May, 1798, on the tiny islet of St. Marcou, which lies four miles from the French coast between Cape Barfleur and Point Perce. A garrison of some 400 Marines and seamen, under the command of Lieutenant Price, R.N., repulsed an invasion mounted by some 9,000 French soldiers from the army assembled at La Hogue especially to throw them out and stop their successful harrassment of French coastal shipping.

Lieutenant Price later described this brilliant little action in stirring tones: 'The gun brigs remained to batter within about three or four

The last fight of Captain Ludlow Strangeways aboard the *Glatton*. (From the print by Henry Singleton, R.M. Museum).

hundred yards, and the flats (landing vessels) rowed up with great resolution, until they were within musket shot; when our guns loaded with round, grape or case, for about one hour cut them up in chips before they could retreat; and our fire on the boats attempting to save those sinking must have occasioned great slaughter, as they were crowded with soldiers for the purpose of storming us'.

In 1797 Bonaparte had laid Egypt at his feet and commenced to march upon the Turkish province of Syria. His advance was upon the city of St. Jean d'Acre, on the coast. Here, however, he was met by a resolute defence inspired by the Commodore of the British squadron in those waters, Sir Sidney Smith. He captured a convoy at sea containing the big French siege guns and used them for the defence of the city instead. In one sortie made by the Marines, the gallant Oldfield, now a Major, was killed leading his men into the French trenches. Even Napoleon himself paid tribute to his bravery. The French General Berthier wrote:

> 'The body of Major Oldfield was carried off by our Grenadiers, who brought him to headquarters; but he had expired before their arrival. His sword, to which he done so much honour, was also honoured after his fall; it remains in the hands of one of our grenadiers'.

The siege continued until the 20th May, when the French retreated to Cairo. Among the other Marines who greatly distinguished themselves at Acre was Major Douglas, who had obtained his first commission in the Corps at the age of thirteen!

At the decisive battle of Aboukir on 13th March, 1801, a battalion of 600 Marines was present. It was recorded that their eagerness to get at the enemy led to their suffering heavy losses. This battalion, commanded by Colonel Walter Smith was thanked by General Abercombie after the battle, 'for their gallant conduct in the course of service yesterday'.

The Marines were present in the north also, at Nelson's victory over the Danish fleet at Copenhagen in 1801 and in numerous cutting-out expeditions against French ships. However, despite these successes, Britain was war-weary after six years of battle. There were now some 30,000 Marines serving, but with the signing of the Treaty of Amiens in 1802, their numbers soon fell and Britain handed back all her conquests save Trinidad and Ceylon.

The 'Royal' Marines

Although the peace which followed the Treaty of Amiens turned out to be no more than a short truce in the long series of wars between France and England it was distinguished, for the Marines, in singular fashion. On 29th April, 1802, His Majesty King George III directed that the Corps should henceforth be styled 'The Royal Marines', and that this was 'in consideration of the very meritorious services of the Marines during the late war'.

The uniform of the Royal Marines was changed to scarlet with blue facings instead of the former white facings. Admiral the Earl of St. Vincent, a much loved and honoured leader in the fleet, had this to say of the honour thus bestowed:

> 'In obtaining for them the title of "Royal" I but indifferently did my duty. I never knew an appeal made to them for honour, courage or loyalty, that they did not more than realize my highest expectations. If ever the hour of real danger should come to England, they will be found the "Country's Sheet Anchor" '.

In this the Admiral was speaking from the heart, for the glorious victories obtained during the war had been somewhat marred by the wave of mutinies which had swept the fleet toward the end of the 18th century. These were inspired by Republican sympathisers within the fleet, tainted with the revolutionary spirit of the Continent, and were further fanned by the infiltration into the ranks, even of the Marines, of 'United Irishmen' who sought to ferment unrest by playing on the many justifiable grievances of the men at this time, and turning the resulting reaction to their own devious ends.

40

Admiral Lord St. Vincent. (From the painting by Beechey, National Maritime Museum, Greenwich).

The greatest of these mutinies started in the Channel Fleet on 15th April, 1797. This outbreak was led by seaman Parker and some like-minded companions and although the Marines, in general, stood apart, they were implicated by the mutineers who presented their own demands in the names of the seamen *and* the Marines. Lord Howe went from the Admiralty to negotiate and honourable terms were reached. In June the ships returned to duty, with unpopular officers removed and free pardons received. However this was not at all to the taste of the extremists and further outbreaks were organised in the fleets at the Nore and at Yarmouth which were accompanied by considerable ill-treatment of officers. At Plymouth Barracks the 'United Irishmen' had infiltrated the Marines, and, led by a Marine named Lee, they plotted to blow up the magazines, release the French prisoners and overthrow the Government. Anyone who opposed them was to be killed. Fortunately news of this mutiny leaked out and was reported by an N.C.O. to Colonel Bowater. He promptly took active steps to disarm the men; the four ringleaders, all Irishmen, were tried by court martial and three of them executed there and then. The Marines in the fleet were restrained by the ships' captains from taking such resolute steps, but gradually the mutiny broke up as the Government stood firm. It threatened to break out also in the ships of the Mediterranean Fleet when word reached them, but in fact it did not. Here Admiral Jervis, later Earl St. Vincent, was the commander and he stood no nonsense at all and the mutiny was still-born. Admiral Jervis was also more enlightened than many of his contemporaries and he saw to it that conditions in the ships of his command were much improved, although the Press Gangs still operated.

IT having been reprefented by the Commander in Chief of the Western Diftrict, that fome wicked diffaffected Perfons are endeavouring to Seduce the Soldiers from a Senfe of their Duty, and exciting them by every Infidious Art to reject with Abhorrence our

Glorious Constitution,

WE, the Non-commiffioned OFFICERS of the PLYMOUTH DIVISION of MARINES, think it our Duty, *(tho never fufpected in the fmalleft Degree to fwerve from that FIDELITY and ATTACHMENT which we owe to our SOVEREIGN,)* at the unanimous Requeft of every Non-commiffioned Officer of the refpective Companies, thus PUBLICKLY to declare our Sentiments.

THAT diametrically oppofite to every DIABOLICAL EFFORT OF FRENCH JACOBINISM, WE feel it our DUTY AND INTEREST to Support our KING, COUNTRY, and CONSTITUTION.

THAT in unifon with our BRETHREN of the other DIVISIONS, WE are unfhaken in our LOYALTY, ever ready to Sacrifice our Lives in the Caufe of our COUNTRY, happy under our prefent COMMANDANT, contented with our OFFICERS, and duly impreffed with every Senfe of Gratitude, for his MAJESTY's LATE MUNIFICENCE.—And in order to evince our Sincerity,

A Reward of Ten Guineas,

Will be given by the SERJEANT MAJOR, *(out of our Joint Subsistence)* to any MARINE, or any other PERSON, who will difcover any Perfon or Perfons, who have, or may hereafter endeavour to fow the Seeds of DISCORD among us, by inftilling thofe falfe Principles of French Liberty, with a view to fubvert that ADMIRABLE and ENVIED GOVERNMENT, under which we feel ourfelves HAPPY.

GOD save the KING.

Signed on Behalf of all the Non-commiffioned Officers, at Quarters.

Charles Goldfmith, Serjeant-Major.

Stonehoufe-Barracks, May 29, 1797.

The document by which senior N.C.O.'s of the Marines pledged their loyalty during the mutinies in the fleet during 1797. (R.M. Museum).

Harmony came only just in time, for in 1803 war again broke out and this time Britain was confronted with the greatest test she had so far faced, to combat the might of the French Empire and the ambitions of the Emperor Napoleon.

A Captain of Marines, 1795. (From the print by Ackermann, R.M. Museum).

Officers of the Royal Marine Artillery, 1833. (From a print in *Costumes of the Royal Navy and Royal Marines*, 1833)

The Royal Marine Artillery and Royal Marines Light Infantry

In 1804 the Royal Marine Artillery came into being, and continued as such until 1923. In 1855 the Royal Marines Light Infantry was so designated until 1923. Between these dates, therefore, the thread of Royal Marines history is divided into two strands, becoming one again in the aftermath of the Great War.

The increased size and complexity of naval guns called for an increase in the numbers of skilled men to man these weapons. By tradition, the Marines had never played a great part in the handling of large pieces of ordnance although this role had several times been suggested for them. Ashore there was also a case for the Corps having its own artillery support for its land sorties. Proposals were made for the formation of Marine gunners but nothing had actually been done. The one exception, discovered by Colonel Field, was at New York in 1780 when Major General Patterson actually formed a 'New York Marine Artillery Company' with eighty men.

The practice had continued for detachments of the Royal Artillery to be embarked to man the mortars in the bomb ketches and other small vessels much used for coastal bombardment work in the 18th century. This led to a certain lack of harmony between Army and Navy officers and in 1804 clashes arose over the question of discipline for such units, the army not being subject to naval discipline when afloat. Nelson is said to have added his support to the idea of forming an Artillery force under direct Admiralty control.

Thus, the same year, there was issued an Order in Council, dated August 18th, which read that: 'We do, therefore, most humbly propose

Field Officers of the Royal Marines in 1833. (From a print in *Costumes of the Royal Navy and Royal Marines*, 1833).

that Your Majesty will be graciously pleased to authorise us to give the necessary directions for forming a company of Royal Marine Artillery, in addition to the present establishment of Royal Marines . . .'. And so the Royal Marine Artillery was formed and was to fight with great distinction for more than a century.

They at first had to contend with great difficulties for they were not held in high regard by the Admiralty and it was not until 1817, for instance, that their numbers, which had been increased to four companies with the foundation of the new Woolwich Division in 1805, were doubled to give a total of eight companies and 700 men. Compared with the expansion of the Royal Marines in that same period the R.M.A. was still a very minor force but it soon grew in stature by example and work. It was the R.M.A.'s early pioneering work which led to the foundation of H.M.S. *Excellent*, the Naval Gunnery School.

The R.M.A. however had to wait for over a decade before they were allowed to exchange their red uniforms for the artilleryman's blue. Thus it was not until October 12th, 1816, that the Admiralty instruction was issued which read that: 'The Royal Marine Artillery are to be clothed as the Royal Artillery except for their buttons and hats which are to be the same as those worn by the Royal Marines'. In 1830 the Admiralty reversed this decision and for a time they again wore scarlet but in 1833 the 'Blue Marines' once again adopted their gunners' uniforms and blue remained associated with them until 1923.

The Corps had grown to fourteen companies by the time of the Crimea, and on November 1st, 1859, the Royal Marine Artillery was formed into a separate Division 3,000 strong and work was commenced on the great headquarters barracks at Eastney, Portsmouth, which was completed in 1867.

In a letter of January 30th, 1855, the Admiralty stated that: 'The Corps of Royal Marines may be designated a "Light Corps" and equipped and designated as such agreeably to Your Majesty's regulations for Light Infantry Regiments of the Line, this training being considered best adapted to the nature of the service which the Corps is generally required to perform when employed on shore'. The title of the Corps therefore became The Royal Marines (Light Infantry), while in 1862 it was further re-styled as Royal Marines Light Infantry.

Perhaps the Royal Marines of the period we have just described can be personified in one man, possibly the most distinguished officer the Corps ever had, 'Fighting Nicolls'. Sir Edward Nicolls was first commissioned on March 24th, 1795, as a Second Lieutenant and received his promotion to First Lieutenant less than a year later. In 1803 he performed the

A battery of Royal Marine Artillery practising upon Southsea Common. (From the painting by Daniel Cunliffe, R.M. Eastney).

45

remarkable feat of cutting-out two vessels from a French convoy with only twelve men under him and that same year he also cut out the *Albion* off San Domingo with great heroism. In 1804 Nicolls was at the siege of Curacao when he took part in the storming of Fort Piscardero.

Promoted to Captain on July 25th, 1805, Nicolls took part in the forcing of the Dardanelles in 1807 when he captured the Turkish commodore's personal standard and led the storming of a redoubt on Point Pesquies. He served at the blockade of Corfu and with the Egyptian expedition in 1807 and the following year was instrumental in the capture of the Italian *Volpe* with a single boat.

On May 18th, 1809, during the Baltic operations, Captain Nicolls led 120 Royal Marines in an attack on the island of Anholt. With the loss of one corporal killed and two privates wounded this little band captured the island defended by 250 men of the King of Denmark's regiment and 300 militiamen. Nicolls was then made Governor of Anholt and put the island in a state of defence for which he received the thanks of the Commander-in-Chief, Baltic. Nicolls was made a Major on August 8th, 1810.

He was A.D.C. to Bernadotte, Crown Prince of Sweden, and in 1812 he served in the War with America, being wounded at the head of a party of Cree Indians during the bombardment of Fort Bowyer in 1814. Despite being wounded three times he took the Crees against New Orleans the following year. In August, 1819, Nicolls became a Lieutenant-Colonel having received two swords of honour for his exploits. He retired as a General on full pay in May, 1835, being made a K.C.B. in July, 1855.

During the course of his long and outstanding service life 'Fighting Nicolls' had been in action 107 times and had received wounds in his right leg, body and right arm, a sabre cut on his head, a bayonet in his chest and in his last action he lost the sight of one of his eyes. As one historian was to write, 'His combatant services surely constitute a record not only in the Royal Marines, but in the British Services'.

The Red Barracks at Woolwich, the home of the 'Court' Division 1805-1869. (From a print by A. Arman, S.R.M., R.M. Museum).

Fighting Nicolls, General Sir Edward Nicolls, K.C.B. (From a painting by an unknown artist, R.M.B. Stonehouse).

Against the Emperor

The recurring wars against France reached their climax after the renewal of hostilities in 1803. Napoleon and his well trained *Grande Armée* prepared themselves for the invasion of England but, like many a dictator before him and since, found belatedly that although his troops might lay the Continent at his feet twenty-two miles of water and the Royal Navy denied him his ultimate ambition. However it all took a great expenditure of time and lives and, as so often before, Britain frequently found herself alone, with the rest of the world either neutral, in the enemy camp or subservient. The Spanish joined the French, Austria and Russia were defeated, Prussia made peace with Napoleon, the Danes joined forces with him, Portugal was conquered and finally America also entered the war against Britain. Despite this, the war was fought to a successful conclusion. The Royal Navy mastered every attempt to dispute its control of the sea and finally even managed to spare sufficient vessels to reduce the American frigates to impotence while the main fleets were engaged on more important duties elsewhere. For the Royal Marines the years 1803 to 1815 were years crowded with incident, from which we can only select some highlights.

At sea, the Royal Marines served in great numbers throughout all the great battles. The Corps connection with Nelson was best illustrated by the fact that he wrote of them: 'When I become First Lord of the Admiralty, every fleet shall have perfect battalions of Marines, with their

Sailors and Marines boarding the French corvette *La Chevrette*, 1801.
From the painting by P.G. de Loutherbourg, City Art Gallery, Bristol.

artillery: and commanded by experienced field officers, they will be prepared to make a serious impression on the enemy's coast'.

At the Battle of Trafalgar, fought against the combined French and Spanish fleets on October 21st, 1805, Nelson inflicted a decisive defeat upon his opponents and one which left the position of the Royal Navy secure for over a century. It was a tragedy that he lost his life in doing so. When he was hit, Sergeant Major Secker and other Marines carried him below, where he died. The Royal Marines suffered heavy casualties at Trafalgar. Some ninety-two officers and 2,600 men served at the battle and four officers and 113 men were killed, with more than two hundred wounded.

Among the Royal Marines lost was Captain Adair of the *Victory's* detachment, who was shot while repelling French boarders, and others of the flagship's unit were sliced down by double-headed shot in their very exposed position on the ship's poop deck. 'It was like a hailstorm of bullets passing over our heads on the poop, where we had forty marines stationed with small arms', wrote Second-Lieutenant Roteley. 'It has been stated that Lord Nelson ordered them to lie down at their quarters until wanted; but no such order was given and no man went down until knocked down.'

When the French Admiral Villeneuve, the Commander-in-Chief of the French and Spanish fleets, wished to surrender it was to a Royal Marines officer, Captain James Atcherley, that he first offered his sword, which he declined, thinking it improper for him to accept such a surrender. The scene as the Captain boarded the *Bucentaure* has been described:

50

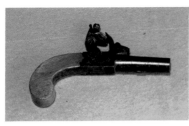

'As the British officer's red coat showed itself on the quarter deck of the French flagship, four French officers of rank stepped forward, all bowing and presenting their swords. One was a tall thin man of about forty-two, in a French Admiral's full dress. It was Villeneuve himself. The second was a French Captain, Captain Majendie, in command of the *Bucentaure*. The third was Captain Prigny, Villeneuve's right-hand man. The fourth was a soldier, in the brilliant uniform, somewhat begrimed by powder smoke, of a brigadier of the *Grande Armée*, General de Contamine, the officer in charge of the four thousand troops serving on board the French Fleet that day.'

Thus passed the epic of Trafalgar, but the war was to last for another ten years, during which the Royal Marines had ample opportunity to gain new honour. From the innumerable actions, major and minor, in which the Royal Marines were involved we give here examples of a coastal raid, a spirited defence, a small-ship action and the campaign in America.

On August 7th, 1807, a cutting-out party was mounted by the seamen and Royal Marines of the *Hydra* against six small craft found hiding in the harbour of Begu, in Catalonian Spain. The harbour was protected by a tower and battery of four 24-pounder guns as well as by marksmen concealed among the scrub in the heights overlooking the port. The *Hydra's* boats nevertheless pressed into the harbour, landed their storming party at the base of the cliffs and, led by Captain Robert Hayes and Lieutenant Edward Pengelly of the Royal Marines, the British party scrambled up the rocks and stormed the fort with bayonet and cutlass. In the dry words of one account, '. . . the garrison cleared out on one side as the stormers entered at the other!' The Marines then held the fort while the seamen took the town and warped out all the shipping despite harrassing fire. Covered by the steady fire of the Marines the party then withdrew with their prizes for the loss of one killed and six wounded. A brisk little action for which Captain Hayes received a Sword of Honour.

The tiny island of Anholt had been taken, as has been related, in 1809, and held by a small garrison. The Danes were determined upon its recapture and the erasing of their earlier humiliation. On March 27th, 1811, in a dense fog at 4 a.m., they landed a force of some 1,600 men to storm Fort Yorke, the lighthouse defence position, and recapture the island. The British garrison at this time consisted of a battalion of 350 Royal Marines and 31 men of the Royal Marine Artillery all under the command of Captain James Maurice, R.N., the new Governor who had replaced Fighting Nicolls. Sir Robert Steele of the Royal Marine Artillery gave an account of the subsequent fighting:

'A heavy fire from the guns of the Masserene Battery, however, soon checked the attack from the south, drove them (the Danes)

51

The gallant defence of the island of Anholt in 1811. (From the print by Lieutenant Richard Turnbull, R.M., R.M. Museum).

over the sandhills for shelter, and blew them out of the one gun battery which they tried to turn against us, and on which they had hoisted their colours.' He goes on: 'The column of attack on the north side met a similar fate; for although the hillocks of sand, breaks and inequality of ground, afforded them protection in their approaches, the Marine Artillery pointed so exactly at the interstices through which the enemy endeavoured to rush into our works, that no forlorn hope could go to more certain death.'

With the two Danish columns halted, reinforcements for the British arrived in the form of an armed schooner with sixteen seamen, the *Tartar* and the *Sheldrake*. The Danes determined on a last great assault but the result was the same.

'Our guns and musketry mowed them down. Melstedt, the Commander-in-Chief, fell by a musket ball, and the next in command, poor Reytz, had both his legs shot away by a cannon ball; and another cannon shot at the same time killed the brave Holstein, who commanded the southern column of attack'. The northern column now held up a flag of truce and, when an adjutant accompanied by a R.M.A. sergeant who could speak the language went out, the Danes asked the British if they would surrender. Told quite emphatically that they would not, the Danes then asked, "Will you allow us to lay down our arms and leave the island?". "Certainly not", was the reply. "Then what terms will you grant?". "None but your unconditional surrender" said the sergeant. This was complied with and this half of the Danish force was locked up. Then the south column undertook to surrender also. Steele goes on to report that: 'When all those who had surrendered had been secured in the stables, a gun was pointed at the door, and a sentinel placed with a slow match, with which he was directed to fire instantly if they attempted to break out'.

Having taken twice their own number as prisoners, the little garrison then harried the remaining 1,000 Danes who were hastily re-embarking at the far end of the island. The Marines had two killed and thirty wounded in this encounter, while the enemy lost 200 dead and 680 captured.

Small ship actions were very numerous and one such in which the Royal Marines played a prominent part was that fought on November 10th, 1808, between the frigates *Thetis* and the French *Amethyst* off L'Orient. A Marine sergeant, Packwood, wrote an account of this action which emphasises the close range of warship actions in the early 19th century:

> 'She had about thirty soldiers in her fore and main tops, and they kept up a constant fire, with their heaving their stinkpots on board; we sustained a very heavy loss about this time, our ship being on fire twice, but was soon put out, and not time to clear the wreck on the quarter-deck. We lay muzzle to muzzle about an hour and ten minutes; our men often stealing their sponges, and the others serving us in the same way; and after an action of full three hours and twenty minutes, she struck after a most obstinate battle, leaving her deck entirely covered with dead and wounded'.

The war against America commenced in 1812 and at first their larger frigates inflicted some heavy losses on the secondary vessels we could spare for that distant theatre. However after H.M.S. *Shannon* had despatched the U.S.S. *Chesapeake* events moved to the land campaigns in which the Royal Marines featured quite largely.

Three battalions with attached artillery were sent out there, seeing much action in the defence of the Canadian border and in raids against the coastal states of America. Washington was burnt as a reprisal for American destruction in Toronto, Baltimore was besieged, but an attack against New Orleans was repulsed by the Americans. Typical of the fighting around the frontier was the capture of Fort Oswego on May 6th, 1814, by a combined force which included the 2nd Battalion Royal Marines, some 400 strong, led by Lieutenant-Colonel James Malcolm. The American fort was situated on a high rocky promontory overlooking the lake and flanked by thick forests filled with American snipers. Landing through heavy fire, including grape shot, the Marines formed into a line with the six companies of De Watteville's Regiment and a company of Glengarry Light Infantry and took the fort at bayonet point inside ten minutes, its defenders, some 500 strong, fleeing to the woods to snipe in safety. Lieutenant Hewett followed Lieutenant Laurie into the fort with the first party, the Marines. Hewett then climbed the flag staff under heavy fire and tore down the American flag and replaced it with the British colours. Despite the fact that he was wounded by several musket balls he reached the ground. A wounded American, who had been spared, attempted to finish him off but a Marine Colour Sergeant saw his move and bayoneted him. Lieutenant Hewett was given the opportunity of taking home the captured flag with despatches but refused to leave while fighting was still taking place.

The steady conduct of the Royal Marines also showed through at the capture of Hampton, when some other regiments gave themselves up to wholesale looting. Sir Charles Napier wrote that: 'Never in my life have I seen soldiers like the Marine Artillery. We suffered much fatigue and hardship, but never was seen anything not admirable in these glorious soldiers. Should my life extend to antediluvian years their conduct at Little Hampton will not be forgotten by me. All honour to the memory of these brave men!'

The great war against Napoleon finished soon after the failure of his last gamble at Waterloo and, with the settlement of Vienna in 1815, Great Britain emerged as the leading nation.

Napoleon inspects the Marines

Although the Royal Marines have fought against every enemy of this country for over three hundred years only once have they come face to face with an enemy head of state. Certainly it must be a rare occurrence for the Emperor of a defeated nation to inspect a guard of honour of his victors but in July, 1815, the Royal Marines were the recipients of this unique distinction.

After receiving his final drubbing at the Battle of Waterloo, Napoleon, with his army in tatters, wrote to the Prince Regent to inform him that, 'I have terminated my political career, and come, like Themistocles, to throw myself upon the hospitality of the British People'. The British People, in their wisdom, having been subjected to fifteen or more years of warfare because of this arrogant French corporal, decided that exile in the safe, and remote, South Atlantic was the limit of their hospitality and he embarked in the battleship *Bellerophon* on July 15th in Rochefort harbour to surrender formally.

The *Bellerophon* sailed the same day for Torbay and Plymouth, where she anchored on the 28th to await the arrival of the battleship *Northumberland* which was to take the Emperor into his final exile with his large retinue.

It was when he first came aboard the *Bellerophon* that Napoleon was received by a Royal Marines Guard. It was a Captain's guard which was turned out to salute him and Napoleon inspected them with great care, passing through their ranks and commenting on their turn out. 'How

Napoleon inspects the Marines aboard the *Bellerophon*, 1815. From the print by V. Huen in *Britain's Sea Soldiers* by Colonel C. Field.

much might be done', he is reputed to have said, 'with a hundred thousand soldiers such as these'. He then requested that Captain Marshall of the Marines put his men through some movements for him to observe and this was done.

When the Guard was brought to the charge Napoleon noticed that, in contrast to French practice, only the front rank charged. He remarked to Captain Marshall that the French method was surely superior, to which Marshall, being a Marine and never lost for an answer, replied that it proved very successful in practice. The Emperor could only reply with a wry smile, "I know that to my cost".

A Marines snuffbox, made from the wood of the frigate *Shannon* and once owned by Colonel J. Phillips. (R.M. Museum).

The Bombardment of Algiers

The Barbary Corsairs of the cities of North Africa had long ravished and pillaged the shores of the Mediterranean and had ventured as far afield as Scandinavia in their raids. Naturally they fell more frequently upon the ships of Spain than of other countries and were therefore, to a large extent, ignored by the other civilised nations who were intent upon their own affairs. However, once Napoleon had been finally dealt with, attention was turned to curbing the activities of these marauders.

Accordingly, Lord Exmouth took the Mediterranean Fleet to the various haunts of these pirates, Tunis, Tripoli and Algiers, offering treaties to the Deys which prohibited the taking of Christian slaves. All agreed save for the Dey of Algiers who was implicated in the massacre of Italian fishermen at Bone. Lord Exmouth was therefore entrusted to mount a punitive expedition and the combined British and Dutch fleets anchored off Algiers on August 27th, 1816. The port was seen to be well defended with forts and guns served by a host of soldiers. Fire was opened

The bombardment of the defences of Algiers, 1816.
(From the print by T. Whitcombe, R.M. Museum).

upon the Allied fleet, to which they replied with devastating effect, the wooden walls of England and Holland completely smashing in and destroying the stone fortifications of the Dey.

The strong Marines detachments aboard the ships were not sent ashore but they served to good effect. The small bomb vessels *Beelzebub*, *Fury*, *Hecla* and *Infernal* were also used against the port's defences, their gunners being four R.M.A. lieutenants, Henry, Maule, James and Bisset, of whom the latter was killed. Another Marines casualty was Captain J. Wilson who had both his legs crushed by a double-headed shot. Despite their subsequent amputation he died shortly afterwards and it is recorded that despite his dreadful injuries he remained calm. On observing a Sergeant Brabazon of the Marines who had lost an arm he is reported to have cheered him with the words, 'Ah Brabazon, are you here? I am sorry to see you thus. There is a glorious work above—we are not unavenged'. The action resulted in the freeing of 1,200 Christian slaves.

Royal Marine Artillery in action covering the rearguard action at the Battle of Hernani, 1837. (From the painting by an unknown artist. C.G.R.M.).

The Spanish Carlist War

This was a not too glorious campaign and the only bright part of it was the conduct of the Royal Marines. The dispute between Don Carlos and his infant niece Isabel resulted in conflict between the 'Carlists' and the 'Christinos', the latter being so called after the Dowager Queen who was served by Government forces. While Don Carlos and his supporters held northern Spain and looked like taking the whole country, the Government forces were hard pressed and would probably have fallen had not England and France intervened with money, men, and, in England's case anyway, by the actual contribution of fighting forces. Unofficially a specially formed 'British Legion' was despatched, comprising two cavalry regiments and ten infantry regiments and from contemporary accounts they were a villainous bunch in all. They were never an effective fighting force and during the frequent skirmishes which took place in the vicinity of San Sebastian during 1836 and 1837 it was only the steadiness of the Royal Marines detachments, landed to assist them, that saved the day and resulted in an eventual Government victory.

This was particularly the case during the Battle of Hernani in March, 1837. The Carlist forces had laid siege to San Sebastian for most of the conflict and it was only the British command of the sea that enabled it to be reinforced. In March a foray was mounted against the siege lines and the Government troops, thanks to the covering fire provided by the Royal Marine Artillery firing spherical case shot, cleared the Carlist trenches and crossed the Urimea. On the 15th an attack was put in against the new Carlist lines at Hernani and once more the fire of the Marines' guns was of paramount importance and the position was taken. Next morning a renewed advance was counter-attacked by the Carlists with considerable effect, the 'British-Legion' giving way to panic and being driven back in some disorder. Time and time again the Royal Marines battalion saved the day, preventing an utter rout and heavy casualties solely by their firmness and steadiness.

An eyewitness in the Royal Engineers small regular detachment was to write: 'You must know the system of fighting here is guerilla, every man for himself, firing as often as you can behind walls, etc. In contrast to this it was beautiful to see the (Royal Marines) battalion throw in a regular fire, as steady as on parade, and Colonel Owen just as cool as in the barrack yard: it was the admiration of all who saw it, and it soon quieted the Carlists. What a fine example of discipline the Marines gave! Had they not acted as they did, our right would have been forced, and the army would have been cut to pieces. They certainly have added another laurel to their many'.

The pity of it was that it was in such a cause, for many felt that Don Carlos had the stronger claim to the Spanish throne. Be that as it may, it

The rearguard action by the R.M.L.I. at Hernani, showing the attack by the Carlists and the last position of the Marines. (From a print by T.L. Hornbrook, R.M. Museum).

The attack on Tinghai, July, 1840. (From the print by Lieutenant White, R.M., R.M. Museum).

was the conduct of the Royal Marines, who never exceeded more than 500 in number, which won the day and, eventually, the campaign. The spirit of the 'Jollies' would seem to have burnt as brightly as ever. One casualty of the Hernani battle was the unit mascot, a dog named 'Dash'. 'Dash' belonged to Captain Bury's company and was in the thick of the fight. During the repulse of a Carlist thrust 'Dash' was hit in the legs but survived, being knighted by a drummer's sword to become 'Sir Dash' for his courage, and he also received a medal made from a Carlist bullet.

The Royal Marines remained on the Spanish coast until August, 1840, when they were withdrawn, but that same year saw the Corps in action again in a limited manner, aiding the Turks against the aspirations of Mehemet Ali who was struggling for Egyptian independence. Prolonged operations resulted in the capture of all the fortresses along the Syrian coast and finishing with the bombardment of the fortress of St. Jean D'Acre in November. The Marines were present during the bombardment by the Allied Fleet but were only called upon to occupy the remnants of the fort and town after the main magazine had exploded causing great carnage among the Egyptian defenders. A few days later a second explosion took place in the magazine with the loss of sixty of the Royal Marines.

A China Campaign

A series of incidents, during which British shipping was threatened by fleets of war-junks and threats were made against British traders, developed, stage by stage, into the first China War. This conflict flared up at intervals between 1840 and 1842 and resulted in the capture of Canton, the forcing of the Boca Tigris defences, the fall of Amoy, Shanghai and other cities to the handful of troops, including small parties of Royal Marines, who operated in the vastness of China with enormous effect.

On the 23rd of May, 1841, after negotiations had been broken off because the Chinese had fired upon a flag of truce, operations to take Canton had been resumed and included in the assault force were 380 Royal Marines led by Captain Ellis. They attacked the forts guarding the northern approaches to the city which almost fell after brief and fierce fighting. Once more there was a truce and the Chinese paid an indemnity while the British re-embarked.

A good example of the type of fighting in which the Marines were involved here was given by an officer from the *Melville* who wrote how 'One house, in particular, which it was necessary to pass, was defended by

The attack on Chuenpee, January, 1841. (From the print by Lieutenant White, R.M., R.M. Museum).

The capture of Canton in May, 1841. (From a painting by an unknown artist, R.M. Museum).

twenty-four men inside, and I endeavoured to get in among them with the idea of saving their lives, or some of them at least; but I got several pokes in the ribs, and blows from their swords. I now got rather hot headed, which being increased by a fellow sticking his spear into my side, whilst ordering the men not to fire, I ran him through the cheek, when he became hot in return, and stabbed the sergeant through the right arm, for which he received the contents of the sergeants fusil through his body, and, after one or two encounters of a similar kind, we captured the fort'.

The last action of this campaign was the storming of the walled city of Chin Keang Foo close to the Yangtse Kiang on 21st July, 1842. The battle took place in blistering heat and some 200 Marines were involved. The walls were stormed and cleared along their whole length with only light casualties, including several, like Major J. Uniacke, a veteran with 38 years service with the Corps, who fell through sunstroke. This proved the final engagement for, with the arrival of the British before Nanking, the Chinese asked for terms.

Lieutenant H. Bradley Roberts. (From a painting by an unknown artist, R.M. Museum).

Against the Russians

The war against Russia which broke out in 1854 was an effort by Britain and France to avert the Czar's encroachment upon the dying Turkish empire. Although known as the Crimea War, operations were in fact conducted against Russia wherever her huge bulk was exposed to British sea-power, which meant the Baltic and the Pacific as well as the Black Sea. Little was done in the Baltic, for the fleet despatched there was ill-manned in general and a great part of its offensive spirit was dulled by the un-justified fear of Russian fortresses. In the Crimea itself Royal Marines infantry and artillery were employed ashore.

The defensive works on the eastern heights guarding the main British supply port of Balaclava were taken over by a battalion of 1,000 Marines commanded by Lieutenant-Colonel Thomas Hurdle, together with 200 more from the battleship *Agamemnon* under Captain Hayes Marriott. This line of trenches, which was to become known as Marine Heights,

The Headquarters of a R.M. Battalion in the Crimea. (From a print by H. Bradley Roberts, R.M.A., R.M. Museum).

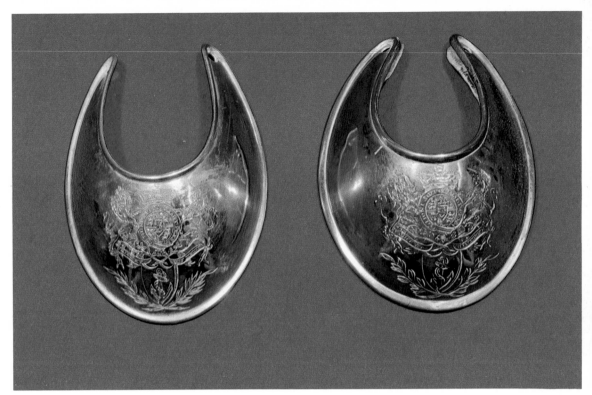

Gorgets 1797-1830. (R.M. Museum).

had some twenty-six guns manned by the R.M.A. They had an opportunity to assist the Heavy and Light Brigades during the famous battle with a covering cannonade against the Russian masses.

It was during the next great Russian thrust against the besieging lines, which resulted in the confused and hard fought battle of Inkerman, that the Royal Marines were again engaged in combat. The Russian columns stormed up the heights in great waves through the fog and mist and were beaten back by resolute fighting by whatever units stood in their line of advance. The Inkerman caves were occupied by Russian snipers and to clear them the Marines were sent in. They cleared the caves with heavy losses and command devolved upon Corporal Prettyjohns and Sergeant Richards when one little group became cut off by an advancing Russian column.

With the ammunition almost gone they drove off their attackers by tumbling the leading Russians down the ridge with heavy stones hurled by Prettyjohns, described as, 'A muscular West countryman'. The awarding of the honours was described by Sergeant N. Turner, 'The Colonel said, "Well, boys, there's only one, but you all deserve one each". The men called out, "Take it yourself Colonel, for you saved all our lives when you ordered us to lie down". "No, no, lads it's for one of you; which shall it be Prettyjohns or Jordan". So they said it should be Prettyjohns. "Then I shall recommend Jordan for the Medal and £20 per annum, for he is in his 21st year of service", said the Colonel.'

Thus it was that the first Victoria Cross to be awarded to a Royal Marine went to John Prettyjohns on 2nd November, 1854. It was not the

Colour Sergeant John Prettyjohns, V.C., R.M. (From a painting by an unknown artist, R.M. Museum).

R.M.A. manning mortars aboard bomb ketches during operations in the Baltic. (From the print by Hamp, R.M. Museum).

An Officer's Coatee 1830-1855, Royal Marine Artillery.
(R.M. Museum).

fate of the Corps to be engaged in any of the other major Crimea battles but this did not prevent them displaying equal courage whenever the opportunity arose. For example during the long drawn-out siege operations against Sebastopol, and in particular during battery work against the great Redan fortress, the Royal Marine Artillery played its part. During counter-battery fire from the Russian defences on 5th June, 1855, severe damage was done to the parapets and embrasures of the British guns and their crews were exposed to a heavy fire without protection. It was Bombardier Thomas Wilkinson who inspired his comrades to repair the shattered defences. Exposed to intense fire from the fortress, he supervised the rebuilding of the earthworks with sandbags until the danger passed. This resulted in the award of another Victoria Cross to the Royal Marines, and yet a third was gained during this war.

As has been noted, only limited operations took place on the Baltic front, but so long a period of inaction aroused the feelings of the press back home and so a number of actions were later undertaken against the smaller forts in the region. On one such occasion Viborg was attacked by a landing party of Marines but they were thwarted by a strong boom defence and the appearance of enemy warships. The swamping of one of the landing cutters would have resulted in her loss to the approaching Russians had not Lieutenant G.D. Dowell of the R.M.A., with three volunteers, bravely gone in after it and towed it clear from under the muzzles of the Russian guns. For this deed he received the Victoria Cross.

On the conclusion of this war, when cold and disease decimated the ranks far more than Russian shells and bullets, the Queen announced, on 2nd February, 1855, that the Corps of the Royal Marines should in future be designated a 'Light Corps', possibly in recognition of their services.

One of the "OLD SCHOOL" doing a bit of "SOLDIERING"

One of the 'Old School' doing a bit of 'Soldiering', at Chatham, 1851. (From a sketch by W.G.R. Masters, R.M. Museum).

The Indian Mutiny

It is a sad fact that although there are a large number of histories of the Indian Mutiny, very few make great mention of the fact that the Royal Marines played a small but vital role in its successful suppression, as part of the famed Naval Brigade led by Captain William Peel, R.N. of the steam frigate H.M.S. *Shannon*. About 150 Royal Marines accompanied the Brigade on its forced march from Calcutta into the interior, fighting as it went.

They fought at Kajwa on November 1st, 1857, having **marched** from Allahabad to Cawnpore and then moved on to raise the siege **of Luckn**ow. In the great storming attacks on the 16th and 17th the tiny **force of 5,000** men assaulted the defences of the Sikandarbagh which it took with great slaughter of the mutineers but were for a time stopped by the Shah Najif position. However this strongpoint was also stormed and carried after severe fighting, during which the few Marines present joined the 93rd Regiment in providing the rebel Sepoys with what they termed a 'Cawnpore dinner' which meant, it is said, six inches of cold steel. The Residency having been evacuated, the force withdrew again to Cawnpore.

At the subsequent battle of Futtegurh in December the Marines approached the vital suspension bridge across the river by boat and helped to put to flight the mutineers who were attempting to dismantle it. After the final fall of Lucknow, the Naval Brigade was withdrawn but another small detachment of Marines led by Lieutenant Pym was instrumental in enabling a body of some 550 men to rout a rebel force of 5,200 in a brisk engagement at Sebanpore on Boxing Day, 1857.

Many years later, one of the Marines recalled a brief skirmish in which he took part in an interview published in the *Globe and Laurel* in 1902.

A mounted officer at Chatham, 24th May, 1850. (From a sketch by W.G.R. Masters, R.M. Museum).

Y^e Trooping Guard at Chatham on Y^e 24th of May 1850.

Royal Marine Artillery, pillbox hat. (R.M. Museum).

Pte. Henry Derry of the R.M.L.I. was with Peel's force when they were ambushed: 'Then Captain Peel led the way to the pits, and in among them he went pell mell, slashing to right and left. I was in disgrace, and was right hand man of the Red Marines. I left the ranks and went after Peel, followed by Corporal Head, who had orders to bring me back. He said that I had one black chiel in my mouth, and one in each hand, banging their heads together. However they soon cleared out, and Corporal Head and I helped Captain Peel, who was quite faint from loss of blood'.

Canton and the Taku Forts

The Second China War had by now broken out and, like the first incident, was sparked off by aggression against British vessels off Canton. The reprisals took the form of the occupation of Canton, followed by a move north against Peking itself. The incident and campaigns dragged on over a period of five years, from 1856 to 1860, the provision of reinforcements being complicated by the Indian Mutiny, which had first call on troops from home.

On the 29th October, 1856, a small party of 199 Marines under Captain Penrose, R.M.L.I., together with some seamen, were involved in an attack against the city walls of Canton and managed to get a foothold inside before being forced to fall back. Further assaults followed and the forts of the city were taken one by one. Because of this the Chinese burnt the British factories on December 14th and so sections of the city were put to the torch in return. The following account gives some impression of the confused skirmishing which was such a feature of the Chinese Wars.

'The Chinese who were maddened by the loss of property and life, manned the house tops to hurl bricks and stones down on our heads, and the Chinese soldiers who were very thick, tried hard to cut us off; but as they had only spears we knocked them down like ninepins. Our party lost two men killed and one mortally wounded. The Chinese got the bodies, and cut off their heads for the reward. We were obliged to make such a sharp retreat that we could not recover their bodies although the Marines offered to go and try.'

In June, 1857, the British, including a force of 250 Marines, attacked and burnt dozens of war junks in the Battle of Fatshan Creek. While the Marines landed and stormed a covering fortress, the sailors destroyed the junks and got involved with the garrison of Fatshan itself. Such few Marines as remained in reserve afloat were then landed and they opened fire on the advancing Chinese hordes, causing their instant withdrawal.

Landing to attack the Taku forts, 1859. (From the
print by W.G.R. Masters, R.M. Museum).

Operations against a city of 3,000,000 people required substantial
reinforcements and in August the 1st and 2nd Battalions, R.M.L.I., with
100 men of the R.M.A., were sent out with Major Travers, R.M.L.I., as
Brigade Major and were joined by a further battalion commanded by
Colonel Lemon, (the Provisional Battalion), from India. With the arrival
of these reinforcements operations for the capture and occupation of the
city went ahead and culminated with its fall in January, 1858. Operations
then shifted to the north when, to prepare for the march against Peking,
the powerful forts guarding the mouth of the Peiho river, the Taku Forts,
had to be taken. This was done fairly simply and their capture resulted in
a peace treaty which was signed in September of that same year.

This treaty was soon broken by the Chinese and they also heavily
reinforced and strengthened the Taku Forts, which they had been allowed
to re-occupy. Thus when hostilities again broke out the forts once more
became the first objective of the British assault. This attack went in on
25th June, 1859, and was made by the 1st Battalion, R.M.L.I., 400 strong,
with another battalion of Marines from the fleet. Although the Marines
commander, Colonel Lemon, protested strongly, the Admiral sent the
attack in against the south wall by boat. A preliminary bombardment by
eleven gunboats was thought to have silenced the forts' 58 guns, but in
fact the Chinese had merely stopped firing to wait for better targets,
which were soon provided.

The Marines were landed from their boats and had to cross several
hundred yards of mud, three deep water-filled ditches and bamboo-spiked
defences, before they reached the walls themselves. The result was
appalling, for the floundering assault party was cut to ribbons. As

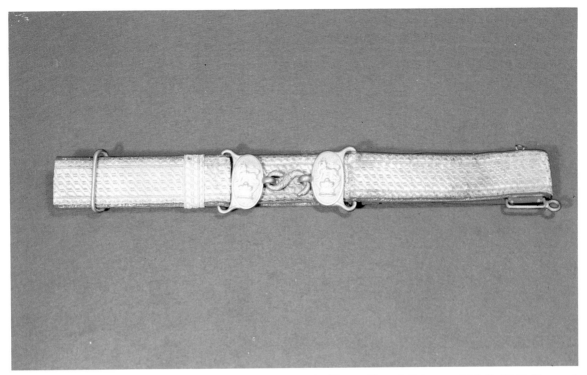

Royal Marine Artillery, officers full dress waist belt. (R.M. Museum).

Colonel Field recorded, 'Not 150 men reached the second ditch, and only fifty the third, at the foot of the ramparts. Their cartridges had been soaked in crossing the previous ditches, and the men were unable to use their rifles'.

A single scaling ladder was valiantly thrown up and ten men attempted to force the great fortress, eight were hit and the ladder thrown down. The force was then evacuated with great difficulty from an impossible position. In the midst of this debacle the heroism of the Marines stood out, like that of Lieutenant H.L. Evans, R.M.L.I., who returned three times into the morass under constant fire to bring out wounded comrades. Because this encounter was a defeat, Evans did not receive a decoration, although it was said at the time that many a man won a Victoria Cross for less.

Towards the end of 1859 the brigade was formed into a single battalion and the following year went to Chusan and Shanghai. By August, 1860, a more formidable force had been assembled under the command of Sir Hope Grant which took the Taku Forts in the rear. The Chinese Army was routed at the battle of Kaowle and 400 Marines were part of the occupation force held outside the walls of Peking until November, when the Chinese Government ratified the Peace Treaty and the British and French again withdrew their forces.

The whole series of campaigns had cost the Corps 232 killed and 222 wounded and at Hong Kong the departing Marines erected a memorial to their fallen comrades. The Marines had not yet finished with the Chinese, however, and two companies continued to serve ashore at Shanghai during the Taiping Rising. Nor were they to have heard the last of the dreadful Taku forts.

Operations in Japan

Although the wall of 'no contact' that the Japanese nation had erected around itself for many centuries was broken down in the mid 19th century there were still many in this still largely medieval society who were strongly opposed to the intrusion of any foreigners whatsoever, especially among the warrior caste, the Sumarai. It was not altogether surprising then that, in July, 1861, some of these fanatics, known as 'Ronins', attacked a British Legation in Yedo and murdered several of the guards. This was repeated in June of the following year, while in September a British merchant was slain because of his bad manners towards the powerful Prince of Satsuma.

With tension mounting a show of force was determined upon and on the 11th August, 1863, an Anglo-Dutch squadron of warships attacked the city of Kagoshima and destroyed its forts and ships. Despite this, agitation against the British grew and reinforcements were called on to

A Japanese cannon captured at the Battle of Simon-oseki, 1864. (C.T.C. Lympstone).

72

Royal Marine Artillery, full dress pouch 1864-1923.
(R.M. Museum).

protect the Legation at Yokohama. In December, 1863, therefore, an R.M.L.I. battalion, eight companies strong from all four Divisions, was sent out from Plymouth aboard the battleship *Conqueror* which had her main armament removed to provide accommodation for the Marines. As Major-General Moulton points out she was, in effect, a forerunner of the *Bulwark* and other commando ships of today.

They camped above Yokohama and were later joined by Army detachments. This force proved itself the necessary deterrent, for it was only called upon to go into action once, when another noble, Prince Chosiu, attempted to blockade the Inland Sea. A combined English, French, Dutch and American squadron was therefore despatched to deal with him in October, 1864, and the Royal Marines Battalion sailed with them aboard the *Conqueror*. A bombardment saw the abandonment of the Prince's forts at Simonoseki and the landing of a force, including Royal Marines under Colonel C. Penrose and another from the fleet under Colonel C.W. Adair, with Major Wolridge as Brigade Major, a Royal Naval Brigade and some Dutch Marines. There was no resistance to their first advance and the Prince was soon asking for terms.

On the Allied forces' withdrawal, however, they were fired on from a stockade hidden in a ravine which overlooked a marshy valley surrounded by thick woods. With the Marines on the left hand side of the valley and the sailors on the right the Allied party stormed the stockade and took it after a brief skirmish. Major W.H. Poyntz, R.M.L.I., later recalled the fight.

> 'I don't know how often I did not fall down myself while endeavouring to make my way too quickly through the thick cover and brushwood towards the stockade. This was built of very strong wooden stakes, having barrack buildings inside, and a large entrance gate in front. However, eventually I found myself, with many others, over the obstruction, after a terrific scramble; while the warriors had an easy exit from the rear of the work by rushing out into the woods which clothed the hill directly behind it. Several were clad in armour, and I have now a couple of suits taken off two defunct men, one chain and the other plate!'

The Royal Marines thus established their mark in Japan and were not called upon to repeat the exercise. The original battalion left in September, 1865, but a second unit, under Lieutenant-Colonel Richards, replaced it between 1870 and 1875 by which time the Japanese had put their own house in order. Before this garrison marched out the battalion was received by the Mikado. The Marines were not to serve in Japan again for seventy years, by which time their medieval foe had become one of the world's greatest powers.

The Ashanti War

The British territories on the west coast of Africa had been cleared of the slave traffic in the early years of the 19th century and life had since proceeded largely untroubled, with ships of the Royal Navy on watch and a small garrison, consisting chiefly of native troops, to keep order. The ghastly climate and the high incidence of disease made the War Office wary of keeping British troops there. In consequence the peaceful coast lay, to a large degree, open to attack from the fierce, wild tribes of the interior. Such an occasion arose in 1873 when King Koffee, the leader of the savage Ashanti Kingdom, with its capital of Kumasi deep in the forests, claimed that the sale of Castle Elmina on the Gold Coast by the Dutch to the British was not legal. To back his claim he sent in an invading army of some 12,000 tribesmen who were initially opposed by only a handful of local troops.

Help came with the arrival of 110 Marines under Captain and Brevet-Lieutenant-Colonel Francis Worsley Festing, R.M.A. who, with Marines and seamen from the warships off the coast, landed and engaged an Ashanti force threatening Elmina. The local population had been so overawed by the fierce warriors that they had been aiding and abetting and as no reply was received to an ultimatum for them to stop, they were bombarded and Kingstown, the trouble spot, was set on fire. This led to an attack by 2,000 Ashanti warriors which was defeated by Festing's force and chased off into the bush.

In October General Sir Garnet Wolseley arrived at Elmina and his first action was to lead a column into the bush against Essamen where a large Ashanti army was encamped. Despite the fact that the British were taunted that the whites would not dare enter the bush, Wolseley's column, including 160 Royal Marines, set off into the interior on 14th October, 1873.

The march through the thick jungle was undertaken and Essamen was found deserted. All the time the column was fired on by invisible warriors at close range, nonetheless they pressed on to the next settlement, Amquana, with the Royal Marines leading in extended order through the bush. Colonel Evelyn Wood, V.C. gave a graphic picture of the conditions in which the Marines fought this war.

> '. . . the operations were carried on in dense forest of gigantic trees, often 200 feet high, laced together with creepers supporting foliage so thick as to shut out the sun. There were few flowers, but, except around villages, the undergrowth was not so thick as near the coast. It was, however, close to villages that most of the fighting occurred, where the system of African cultivation afforded good cover to our enemies.'

As the column approached Amquana it was again attacked by unseen guns and some of the native infantry became nervous and fired off their guns into the bush and sky. They were eventually steadied and the Marines and seamen advanced into the forest on either side of the line of advance and cleared the approaches of the enemy with steady fire. Thus

Fighting in the Ashanti forests, 1873. (From a painting by Charles Stadden, R.M. Museum).

Amquana fell and the Ashanti moved back further from the coast until they were hemmed in their own lands. A final expedition was then mounted which resulted in their final defeat and the burning of Kumasi. By this time further reinforcements had arrived, including a battalion of Royal Marines, but these were kept in their ships, and only those Marines accompanying the Naval Brigade got into Kumasi.

In truth the climate was equally as deadly as the Ashanti warrior, but in recalling the defence of Abrakrampa in November, Wolseley paid tribute to the Royal Marines by stating that it was due solely to the admirable conduct of Major Russell and his fifty Marines that the town was held against an attacking Ashanti army of 10,000 warriors for two days. Thus in the steamy forests of the 'White Man's Grave' did the Royal Marines uphold their proud traditions, although such a type of action probably did not occur to any of them when they had joined up to fight with the Queen's Navy afloat.

Tel-el-Kebir

The violent nationalism of Arabi Pasha, the Egyptian Minister of War, had, in 1882, led to him being almost the military dictator of the country with the Khedive powerless to oppose him, and a massacre of unfortunate European civilians in the streets of Alexandria ensued. The Mediterranean Fleet, under Admiral Seymour, arrived to watch over British subjects but the French backed out. When the Egyptians started to mount heavy guns to command the harbour Seymour issued a warning and when it was ignored the fleet carried out a bombardment which destroyed the military installations and forced the Egyptian army to flee. A Royal Marines force, commanded by Colonel H.B. Tuson, arrived with the Channel Fleet and had a hard and thankless task in restoring order in Alexandria where the rioting mob had complete control. This done, the British had to restore the Khedive and General Sir Garnet Wolseley was appointed to carry out the task. In August, as part of the build-up of forces, a second Royal Marines battalion, under Lieutenant-Colonel S.J. Graham, arrived in Egypt. Feints were made by both these forces which resulted in the seizure of Ismailia and Port Said and by September Wolseley was ready to make the decisive move by crushing the Egyptian army which held strongly fortified lines at Tel-el-Kebir, covering Cairo.

The Royal Marines had been engaged in three skirmishes, at Mallaha Junction on 5th August, and twice at Kassassin on the 28th August and 9th September, when two guns were captured intact by the R.M.L.I. For the major operation the two battalions were joined to the 2nd Brigade commanded by Major-General G. Graham, V.C., C.B. As the British army

Working a captured gun mounted on a railway truck at the Battle of Kassassin, 1882. (From the painting by Colonel C. Field, R.M. Museum).

advanced, the Egyptians counter-attacked on the 9th September but were routed with heavy losses and pursued back to their trenches. Many Marines wanted to continue the pursuit but General Wolseley wished to make his main attack, when it came, a decisive one, and thus wished the enemy to hold fast until he could destroy him completely. And thus it came to pass for, on the night of the 12/13th September, the British marched forward to within striking distance of the formidable defence works of Tel-el-Kebir and, as first light broke in the sky, the attack went in.

The R.M.L.I. formed the left hand sector of the 2nd Brigade's line and vied with the Highland Brigade in being the first into the Egyptian trenches. Colonel C. Field, R.M.L.I. was present at the battle and described the actual attack as he saw it in the line of advance.

> 'It seemed to me that the Egyptian lines were 800 to 1,000 yards distant, and this being the case, we were ordered to lie down and fix bayonets. Four companies were then extended as a firing line, followed by the remaining four as supports. We advanced by rushes, lying down to fire. The enemy's bullets were still falling thickly and the entrenchments and our own firing line still blurred with smoke when the bugles — to the relief, I think, of everybody — sounded the 'Charge'. The whole line, every man burning to get at the Egyptians, rushed forward at the double with a continuous shout or roar rather than a cheer. As we caught a misty outline of the parapet at a few yards distance there was a slackening of fire — our firing line had at that moment rushed it, followed closely by the supports, and after a minute or two's play 'with the baynit and the butt' that part of the works was ours.'

Both wings of the British Army took the trenches in that rush and the Egyptians, who stood their ground for a while, suffered heavy losses and then broke. While fleeing from their fortifications they were cut off by the cavalry and were cut to ribbons. This decisive battle cost the Marines some thirteen killed including Major H. Strong and Captain Wardell. The cavalry entered Cairo next day and the Khedive was reinstated. The two Marines battalions sailed for home on 19th October.

The Battle of Tel-el-Kebir; Royal Marines celebrate
their victory. (From the painting by Colonel C. Field,
R.M. Museum).

An R.M.L.I. officer's Shako, 1869-1878. (R.M. Museum).

Overleaf:
A halt at sunset by the Guards Camel Regiment in the Bayuda Desert. The Royal Marines contributed one company to this composite unit in 1885. (From the painting by Bartelli, 45 Commando, R.M.).

Royal Marines Light Infantry in action at the Battle of Tamaii, 1884. (From the painting by Charles Stadden, R.M. Museum).

Against the Mahdi

After the defeat of the Egyptian army by the British, the Dervishes of the Sudan rose up and commenced a campaign of murder and pillage, led by a carpenter's son named Mohammed Ahmed who proclaimed himself Mahdi the prophet, come to clear the Egyptians and infidels from the land. Promising the faithful immunity during battle and an equal share of everything gained after victory, he soon raised the whole of the Sudan in revolt and, in 1883, he completely annihilated an Egyptian army at El Obeid, while a second Egyptian army suffered the same fate at El Teb the following February.

Meanwhile Royal Marines had been landed from the ships of the East Indies Squadron to secure the Red Sea port of Suakin, and were joined later by a further battalion from the Mediterranean Fleet who were attached to the 2nd Brigade, commanded by Sir Gerald Graham. The Brigade assembled at Trinkitat, the Marines being commanded by Major G.H.T. Colwell. The force advanced against the 'Fuzzy-wuzzy' positions at El Teb in square formation on 29th April, 1883, passing over the scene of the earlier carnage as they did so. The Marines, 380 strong, were positioned on the left face of the square which moved in to attack the left flank of the Mahdi's forces entrenched on the hills above. This involved a flanking march during which the Royal Marines were on the exposed side of the square.

The square then advanced upon the enemy positions under heavy fire but when almost upon them the Dervishes rose up in thousands and charged down the hill. They were met by a steady fire from the square which decimated their ranks, but the fanatical survivors threw themselves at the front lines' bayonets in an effort to break through, believing

themselves invulnerable to death. The survivors retreated and massed around their wells and central positions and it required much hard fighting to break them. The Mahdi General, Osman Digna, is said to have explained away the loss of 3,000 of his 6,000 men by saying that he had, by mistake, given his troops the wrong fetish against steel and lead!

The Dervishes were still defiant and another large army was assembled at Tamaii. On being asked to submit to the rule of the Egyptian Government they declared their intention to continue the fight and so a second British attack was decided upon. The Royal Marines Battalion now had fourteen officers and 464 men in six companies under Colonel H.B. Tuson, R.M.A., and when the advance commenced against Tamaii on the 10th March, 1884, they formed the base of the fighting square. When the final advance began across the valley towards the Dervish camp the British forces were formed in two squares, with the Marines in the 2nd Brigade's square. It was on this formation that the main Dervish attack fell and such was the weight and power of their charge that the square broke and was pushed back for 800 yards with some casualties. It was at this critical juncture that Major Colwell, R.M.L.I., was heard shouting 'Men of the Portsmouth Division, rally'. And to their credit 150 of them did, forming a small square. Gradually the position was resolved and the main square reformed while the attacking Dervishes were enfiladed by the 1st Brigade and the dismounted Hussars. The attack was resumed and the camp of Osman Digna burnt before the British marched back to Suakin. The Marines spent the rest of the year as part of the garrison holding Suakin, based in makeshift forts.

The British Government had, however, no firm intention of settling accounts completely with the Mahdi and recommended instead the complete withdrawal of the Egyptians from the land, and General Gordon in Khartoum began to supervise it. However, it was not long before he was cut off and unable to escape with what forces remained. An attempt to break through to him was therefore mounted which led to the Nile Campaign of 1884/5. General Wolseley decided to try and reach Khartoum from the Nile instead of from Suakin and accordingly he advanced in two columns, a River Column, supported by gunboats, and a Desert Column, which included the Guards Camel Regiment of four companies, one of which was provided by the R.M.L.I. Towards the end of the year this column was despatched to cut across the Nile loop and reach Gordon as an advance guard. They had to fight hard for the vital water wells of Abu Klea but, although victorious, they reached the Nile at Metemneh too late to save Gordon who had by then been murdered.

It was during this campaign that the men of the R.M.L.I. became familiar with the 'ships of the desert'. Alexander Macdonald gave the first verse of a song composed by the Marines poet, one Sergeant Eagles, which was sung around the campfires at Wadi Halfa:

'When years ago I listed, Lads, To serve our Gracious Queen,
The sergeant made me understand, I was a Royal Marine,
He said sometimes they served in ships, and sometimes served
on shore,
But never said I should wear spurs, and be in the Camel Corps,
I've rode in a ship, I've rode in a boat,
I've rode in a railway train,
I've rode in a coach and I've rode a moke,
And hope to ride one again;
But I'm riding now an animal, A Marine never rode before,
Rigg'd up in spurs and pantaloons, as one of the Camel Corps'.

And they really *were* issued with spurs.

Before the Sudan was finally abandoned, the R.M.L.I. fought two more fierce battles against the Dervishes near Suakin. On 20th March they stormed the enemy hills of Hasheen with the Berkshire Regiment in what was described as, 'making it look like a race between the two Corps to reach some hillocks on the right of the ridge'. On the 23rd March these two battalions were taken by surprise by the Dervishes at McNeill's Zareba and their squares were broken. Lieutenant F.G. Cotter described the wild Dervish attack: 'While thus employed we were all suddenly startled by a roaring noise just like the sea would make in a squall. A cry of "They're upon us" and "Stand to your arms" was raised. The Cavalry scouts came galloping in immediately followed by a mass of Arabs.' Quickly reforming, they rallied and drove off the enemy with heavy losses. This column was harried all the way back to Suakin, another officer remembering how 'They never think of turning but come right on till killed'.

With the end of the campaign the Sudan was left in the grip of the Mahdi's successors, for he had died at the end of the year, but his followers made his tomb the centre of their faith and continued to attack, at intervals, the Egyptians and other neighbours. Thirteen years were to pass, however, before these savage tribes were to face the final reckoning.

The Sudan

In March, 1896, a new event so inflamed the Dervishes that the security of Egypt was again put to the test. In March an Italian army had been totally defeated by the Abyssinians at Adowa and this set the tribes in a ferment. Luckily the intervening years had seen the Khedive's army trained by the British into a much more workmanlike force than that which had suffered at the hands of the Dervishes in 1883. So when the British Government finally decided upon a punitive expedition to reconquer the Sudan they had a sound basis for their army and the Royal Marines were not greatly called upon to participate. However Royal Marines officers did give aid to Kitchener for, at the decisive Battle of Omdurman, Captain H. Slessor, R.M.A. commanded the 1st Egyptians, Captain G.E. Matthews, R.M.L.I. the 14th Sudanese and Lieutenant-Colonel Townsend the 12th Sudanese battalions.

Apart from officers such as these the only Royal Marines to take an active part in Kitchener's advance up the Nile were those under Captain H. Oldfield, R.M.A. who, with nine corporals and bombardiers, was sent to Egypt in June, 1896, to train and supervise the Egyptians who manned the guns of the little fleet of gunboats which accompanied the army's advance. They saw considerable fighting and were frequently in the thick of the vanguard actions. One of them was commanded by a certain Lieutenant Beatty, R.N. who later became Admiral of the Fleet, Earl Beatty, commander of the Battle Cruisers and, later, of the Grand Fleet during the Great War.

A R.M.L.I. Officer's Forage Cap, of 1880. (R.M. Museum).

Although they were only represented by a handful of men, the Royal Marines succeeded in making their mark upon the campaign, as, for example, when Colour Sergeant Jenvey, R.M.A., quitted the gunboats and accompanied a Naval Rocket Party during an attack on the Dervishes' camp. He later related how, 'On account of the distance and nature of the ground, I was unable to get in any good work with the rockets, so the General gave us permission to move to the right of the artillery, and we took up a good position at 500 yards range, where I was able to get in some good shots, setting their camp on fire in several places'.

As a final postscript to this campaign Corporal Maynard, R.M.A., assisted in placing the explosive charge which destroyed the Mahdi's tomb, 'together with a few of the faithful!'

Fighting the Boers

When the war in South Africa, the Second Boer War as it has become known, erupted in October, 1899, the British garrison at the Cape was initially heavily outnumbered and was also outranged by the Boer artillery. Luckily the warships on the station included the cruiser *Terrible* from which that brilliant gunnery officer Percy Scott was able to organise a Naval Battery with 4.7-inch guns which operated to good effect. Although this war was fought on a substantial scale Royal Marines were not heavily involved. The employment of the Marines afloat had gradually become more and more a case of their being utilised as additional gun crews, and, further, the reaction of the other European nations, led by Germany and Holland of course, was violently opposed to the British defence of the Cape so it was felt wiser for the Royal Navy and Royal Marines to concentrate their energy in securing the sea links and preparing against any possible intervention by one of the Great Powers. Thus the land fighting was left almost entirely to the army.

However the Royal Marines, as usual, were not completely absent from the fighting and at the Battle of Graspan they were in the fore. On November 19th the seamen and Marines from H.M. Ships *Doris*, *Powerful* and *Monarch*, which had been sent to Stormberg, were organised at Simonstown. The Marines formed a R.M.A. company of fifty men and two R.M.L.I. companies, totalling 190, and, together with a naval battery of four 12-pdr guns, they were moved north by rail to reinforce Lord Methuen's relief column attacking toward Kimberley, thus supporting the army in the battle at Belmont. On the 25th November, 1899, the advancing force came up against the next Boer line on the kopjes at

Graspan. After a preliminary bombardment the Marines were sent in with the seamen on the flank of the King's Own across the open veldt against their hidden enemy, in a series of rushes in extended line, four paces apart. In such a tight formation they gave the Boers a good target and their losses were severe. Lieutenant W.T.C. Jones, R.M.L.I., later wrote in the *Globe and Laurel* of the attack.

> 'There was not the slightest cover for the attacking force, the flat veldt extending some thousands of yards round the positions; the grass on the veldt was about 18 inches high, with an occasional anthill here and there.'

The Marines deployed in single rank at 7 a.m. and started forward and, at 7.45 a.m., the main guns ceased firing.

> 'We were 700 yards from the base of the principal kopje when the guns ceased firing, and almost immediately the kopjes, which a moment before had seemed quite clear of the enemy, opened a regular storm of fire'.

Another R.M.L.I. officer, Lieutenant the Rt. Hon. Leslie O. Wilson, also recalled this moment:

> 'The men fell quickly after the first rush, Captain Senior, R.M.A., being killed in the second rush, and Major Plumbe in the last rush before reaching the foot of the kopje, just as he had stood up to give the signal to advance. When we reached the foot of the kopje we were in comparative safety, out of sight of the enemy. Our men then rushed the position with fixed bayonets, but by the time they reached the top of the kopje, all the Boers had fled in carts or horseback carrying their dead and wounded with them.'

This costly advance across open country resulted in the loss of eight killed and eighty-three wounded out of the Marines total of 190 officers and men. The Marines were not engaged again in a major battle and the war gradually took on a guerilla aspect until its termination in 1902.

Action against the Boxers

The rising of the Chinese 'Boxers' in 1900 came about, it is thought, by the designs of the Prefect of Tsau Chaou who raised this body, also known as the 'Patriotic Harmony Fists', to threaten the corrupt Manchu Dynasty, but so rapidly did the movement spread across the land and so virulent was its outlook against all 'foreign devils' that the lives of the foreign communities in China were soon at grave risk. The Chinese government itself was quite content to stand aside and allow the passions of this popular organisation to turn upon the foreigners rather than on themselves and it was quickly apparent that strong measures would have to be taken by the military on the spot.

On the 31st May the 'Winter Guard' for the legations at Peking marched through the great city gates, the British detachment consisting of three officers and 79 men of the R.M.L.I. and some naval ratings. As they marched in, through streets lined with thousands of sullen Chinese, their guide remarked that he did not think the Guard would return by the same route as the one they had entered by. On being asked which way they would return the guide shook his head, looked to the sky and replied 'You go up top!' Nor were his words idle threats, for reports that the Boxer rebels were closing in on the city were received and by June 13th they were in Peking. All the legations were clustered together just outside the walls of the Imperial City and inside the massive walls of the Tartar city, while the extension of the Chinese city to the south further isolated them. Plans were made by all the nationalities present, comprising the British, Germans, Americans, Japanese, Russians, Italians and

Captain L.S.T. Halliday, R.M.L.I. who won the Victoria Cross in the fighting at the Peking Legations in 1900. (From the painting by Major W.G. Goldsmith, V.R.D., R.M.R., R.M. Museum).

Austrians to make a common defence against attack. On June 19th, the
Imperial government issued them with an ultimatum to leave. As this
would have entailed the men, women and children leaving their sanctuary
to reach the coast through a land filled with thousands of Boxers this
would have led to a massacre. The German minister left the legations to
put this point to the Chinese government but was murdered by his
Chinese escort on the way. The tiny garrison then settled in for a siege.
Luckily there was no lack of fresh drinking water, although soon the
community was reduced to eating horse-meat. There were pitifully few of
them in the vast city but barricades were erected and makeshift cannon
were constructed. Fortunately the Boxers were content to starve them out
slowly, only making piecemeal attacks from day to day despite their huge
numbers. The garrison kept up a vigorous defence, and from time to time
they sortied out against their besiegers, the Royal Marines and the U.S.
Marines fighting side by side.

During one such action on June 24th Captain L.S.T. Halliday, R.M.L.I.,
led a section of twenty of his men through the wall to drive off a Boxer
attack. In his own words he, 'Went down a narrow alley and came upon
five men with rifles round the corner of a house. One immediately plugged
me in the shoulder cutting the left brace of my Sam Browne belt in half. I
then began to empty my revolver into them; as they were only a yard
away there was no question of missing. I finished four and the fifth bolted
round another corner'.

In actual fact Captain Halliday had been hit by a bullet which fractured
his shoulder and took away part of his lung. Corporal William Gregory
was part of this little force and he recalled how, 'Private Sawyer was most
seriously wounded in this affair, and others had marvellous escapes.
Private Layton had his serge and trousers both shot through without the
bullet touching his skin. I got my bayonet smashed by a bullet; it is
wonderful that none of us were killed in this affair'.

By this time the Imperial troops had joined forces with the Boxers.
They had earlier stood by on the city walls while the Boxers slaughtered
every Christian Chinese they could lay hands on and burnt entire quarters
of the Chinese city. But still they did not make an all-out attack on the
Legations.

Meanwhile help had been sent up by rail. A force consisting of some
2,000 men from the International fleet at the mouth of the Peiho river, and
including some 213 Royal Marines, was led by Vice-Admiral Sir Edward
Seymour, the British Commander-in-Chief. They set out on June 9th but,
within 25 miles of the city, they found the lines torn up before and behind
them and a large army barring their way. They had to fight their way back
on foot and while trying to pass by the Hsiku arsenal, some ten miles from
Tientsin, early on the morning of 21st June they came under heavy fire.

Sergeant Cooper, R.M.L.I., later wrote that, 'They hailed us across the water: "Who are you and whither you go?" We answered that we were foreign troops making our way to Tientsin, and the reply came back, "It is well". Hardly had the words sounded before the stillness was broken by a roar of musketry, and the whole line of parapet flashed into a sheet of flame. We were caught in a sort of death trap, and for an instant all was confusion'.

In this desperate position it was the Royal Marines who broke the impasse. Major J.R. Johnstone took his detachment back up the road, crossed the river and made a bayonet attack against the rear of the arsenal which drove the Boxers out. The whole party then took sanctuary in the arsenal and were in turn put under siege.

Nor were things better down river at Tientsin itself. Here some fifty or so Royal Marines under Major E.V. Luke and Lieutenant H.G. Armstrong, together with seamen, German, French and Russian troops, were ready to defend the concessions from the Boxers. An attack was made on the French holding the railway station, which they beat off. The great International fleet was below the grim Taku forts which had been further strengthened in the intervening years and now mounted modern artillery pieces. In addition, four German-built destroyers were moored close by manned by Chinese seamen. It became apparent that the rebellion was spreading and to forestall the Boxers gaining the forts an ultimatum was issued calling for their withdrawal. This was answered by a Chinese bombardment to which the fleet made reply and landed troops who took the forts. Because of this the regular Chinese army now threw in its lot with the Boxers and heavy fighting developed.

It was not until August 4th that a sufficient force was gathered to form an International army of 20,000 men which fought their way through to Peking to raise the siege on the 14th. Prior to this both Tientsin and Hsiku had been relieved but it was too late for Captain B.M. Strouts, R.M.L.I., who was killed on July 15th leading his Marines at the Legations. The day before another Marine, Sergeant J.E. Preston, R.M.L.I., had earned the Conspicuous Gallantry Medal by capturing a Boxer standard while clearing the wall.

Pax Britannica

The hundred years between the end of the Napoleonic Wars and the opening of the Great War saw the Royal Navy exhibiting its strength throughout the globe in the interests of peace. Although conflicts erupted from time to time, as we have seen in the preceding pages, there were other incidents of a minor nature when the suppression of slavery, action against rebels, or policing work about the Empire brought the ubiquitous Marine Corps into action. There is not space to describe them all but here we can mention a few.

When Mehemet Ali, a tobacconist who had risen to become Pasha of Egypt, invaded Syria and defeated the Turkish army, the Great Powers, who had no wish to see the Ottoman Empire crumble, intervened. The Mediterranean Fleet landed its Royal Marines near Beirut and there were eventually about 1,500 of them concentrated there in two battalions. They were led by Colonel W. Walker and extra drafts from home raised their numbers to a brigade. Under the irrepressible leadership of Sir Charles Napier, sailor turned general, they took Sidon and Tyre, and bombarded and occupied Acre which led the Egyptians to make a hasty peace at the end of 1840.

Operations against the Maoris in New Zealand started in 1843 and were resumed from time to time until they were finally pacified in 1870. The Royal Marines took part in several sharp actions against these hardy

The landing at Tortola on the Syrian coast in 1840 by Royal Marines from H.M. Ships *Carysfort* and *Zebra*. (From the painting by Robert George Kelly, R.M. Museum).

warriors, including Heke's Pah at Okaihu in 1845, Ruapekapeka the following year, Pukitakaneri in June, 1860, and Ta Awamuta in February, 1864.

In South America the Argentinian armies besieged Montevideo and Britain sent troops to protect her interests there. Then at the battle of Puente Obligado on 20th November, 1845, a force of Royal Marines 145 strong under Captain F. Hurdle broke the blockade by storming the enemy batteries which covered the Parana river.

The recurring troubles with the Irish terrorist organisations necessitated the stationing of Marines detachments in Ireland during Queen Victoria's reign, especially during the attempted rebellion of 1848, while similar detachments were sent out in 1868 and 1880 to deal with disorder and attacks on Protestants. If anyone wishes to compare the restraint shown by the Royal Marines in similar circumstances more recently then the following extract from an interview with a Corporal of Marines in 1881 is very revealing:

> 'We had strict orders not to hurt anyone if it could be helped. I have stood for more than an hour with stones whistling about me and many of them hitting me, and never struck a blow. The men were pretty bad, but the women were lots worse. They were like savages with hair flying loose, and generally without shoes and stockings. They knew uncommonly well that we shouldn't touch them, whatever they did, and they took advantage of it to any extent'.

On the Gambia river in 1894 a small force under Lieutenant-Colonel A.D. Corbet, R.M.L.I., consisting of 50 Royal Marines and 50 men of the West India Regiment, was attacked in their entrenchments at Subaji by 1,500 Mandigo tribesmen. They were defeated by Corbet and driven back across the river. Further fighting followed and the campaign ended with the destruction of Gunjur. Another small party under Major J.H. Bor R.M.A.[*], policed the island of Crete during a rebellion there in 1896.

In February, 1897, a peaceful mission at Benin was massacred without any cause after the tribesmen had been roused by 'fetish chiefs'. An expedition was despatched to avenge these murders and, under overall command of Rear Admiral Rawson, a small force set off to Benin City. Included in their ranks was a Royal Marines detachment consisting of 100 men of the R.M.L.I. under Captain Byrne and 20 R.M.A. gunners under Lieutenant F.L. Diblee. After fighting at Oglobo and Awoko they stormed the city on the 18th and the King and his retainers fled.

---

[*] *A direct descendent of Colonel Bor who was present at the Capture of Gibraltar.*

One of the worst disasters to befall the Corps during these times was not brought about by the enemy but by an error of judgement by the commander of the Mediterranean Fleet. While carrying out a complicated manoeuvre off the coast of Syria, near Tripoli, on June 22nd, 1893, the flagship, the battleship *Victoria*, crossed close in front of the battleship *Camperdown*. The great underwater ram of the latter, a feature of Victorian battleships, opened up the *Victoria* and she went down with heavy loss of life. The detachment of 98 Royal Marines fell in with perfect discipline on the quarterdeck until the ship capsized ten minutes after being struck. All save thirty were drowned. Their example was as gallant as that courage which had earlier been displayed by the Army when the *Birkenhead* went down, and this similarity was acknowledged in Kipling's lines:

> 'But to stand an' be still to the Birkenhead drill is a dam' tough bullet to chew.
> And they done it, the Jollies—'Er Majesty's Jollies—soldier an' sailor too'.

A Horse Marine! This old print shows King William IV, The Duke of Wellington and Lord Hill. (From a cartoon by MacLean, R.M. Museum).

Indeed Kipling's epic poem to the memory of the Royal Marines, sums up perfectly the role and duties of the Corps during the long high summer of Imperial glory that ended in the mud and on the wire of the Western Front a few years later.

> 'An' after I met 'im all over the world, a' doing all kinds of
> things,
> Like landing 'isself with a Gatlin' gun to talk to them 'eathen
> Kings;
> 'E sleeps in an 'ammick instead of a cot, an' 'e drills with the
> deck on the slew,
> An' ' e sweats like a Jolly—'Er Majesty's Jolly—Soldier an'
> Sailor too!'

One final postscript should be added to this era. When Britain intervened in Mexico in 1861 it was the Royal Marines who provided a mounted detachment to help and so there really were 'Horse Marines' after all!*

Changes and Reforms

Routine duties of the Royal Marines ashore, and more particularly, afloat, changed in the course of the 19th century with an ever-increasing tempo. Whereas the Marine of 1840 would, to a very large extent, carry out duties under circumstances that had not greatly changed since the first Marines of a hundred years earlier, by the 1880's the warship had altered beyond any comparison. These very great alterations in warship design, with steam ousting sail, enormous guns in barbettes and turrets replacing the smaller cannons, the advent in the 1870's of the quick-firing gun and the machine-gun, the huge expansion of the fleet in the first decade of the twentieth century, and the great reforms of that period, all combined to make life in the Royal Marines, outside the highlights of active service, very trying indeed.

There had always been much to complain of in the conditions and equipment of the Marines in comparison with the line regiments. These faults continued into the early years of the 19th century but were gradually eradicated. One problem that did not alter was that of promotion In such a limited Corps, promotion had always been hard to obtain and many officers served for years without any elevation in rank whatsoever. Let us reproduce two examples cited by Colonel Field. Lieutenant-Colonel William McKinnon served as a Subaltern from March 13th, 1809

---

* In fact the term 'Horse Marines' was first adopted when men of the 17th Light Dragoons embarked aboard ships of the fleet in the late 18th century.

to 8th June, 1838, including two years, one month on half pay, a total of 28 years, 10 months. Major-General John Tothill, 8th December, 1808 to 10th July, 1837, one year on half pay, totalling 28 years, 9 months. In 1845 even, of the Captains at the head of the list, two had held Commissions for 43 years, eight for 42 years and ten for 41 years. This state of affairs was reflected in a 'Marines Lament' of 1846:

'In every clime, full many a time, with foes I've had a rub, On sea and land I've made my stand, Yet still I stand a Sub, When, age-oppressed and gout-possessed, our companies we get, Sir,
Some scarce can stand, much less command, We are a luckless set, Sir!''

It is little wonder then that the more ambitious officers left for periods of service elsewhere or transferred altogether, while those that remained were somewhat embittered at the role in which they were cast. Nor was this position improved by the fact that, of necessity, the numbers of Royal

3. - Very good, Sir !

Very good Sir! Strict attention to detail and immediate compliance with orders was a hallmark of the Royal Marines serving afloat at the turn of the century as this wry cartoon noted at the time. (From the cartoon by H. Gervese, R.M. Museum).

Marines embarked in the ships of the fleet became progressively fewer towards the turn of the century, despite the increase in the number of seagoing ships. Marine detachments carried aboard even the smaller vessels, like frigates, had been quite large in Napoleonic times, but the need for the R.M.L.I. to provide massed rifle fire had long been done away with by automatic weapons and by the increasing ranges at which naval actions were intended to take place. Although the involvement of the R.M.A. with the manning of the largest guns of the fleet had been manifest since as early as 1826, when Captain Glascock, R.N. recorded that the Royal Marines had, 'regular instruction and acquaintance with the management of Great Guns', there still remained.the fact that the number of gunners required to supplement the naval personnel was much smaller than before.

Another irritation was that it sometimes happened that, in matters of seagoing discipline, a Marines officer might not have very much control at all over his own men. While the better ships' captains would ensure that in such affairs the Marines officers dealt with the problem, or at least acted through himself, others could relegate such duties to their lieutenants and thus a veteran Marines officer might find himself subordinate to a fresh-faced naval lieutenant.

These differences became further emphasised when the opportunity for regular exercising became more and more hard to obtain. The 'Soldiers and Sailors too', felt that they were treated as merely substitute sailors who got in the way afloat. It is true that new rates were introduced in 1886 and that from this time forward the men themselves were encouraged in the bettering of gunnery aboard ships with some startling improvements in accuracy, nevertheless the officers still felt that they were under-used.

It was unfortunate that in the first decade of the 20th century the unhappy 'New Scheme' of entry was forced upon the Marines, which only added fuel to such discontent. This was the Selborne Scheme brought in by Admiral Fisher whereby common entry was started which would reduce the Royal Marine officers to the same status as executive branch officers in the Royal Navy. This proved so unattractive that in the five year period only two officers who entered via the new colleges of Osborne and Dartmouth went into the Marines and therefore the whole scheme was dropped. In 1912 the old arrangement was resumed.

Although these points jarred upon the Royal Marines during this period it must be emphasised that the 'Jollies' were never overladen with such matters, there was no lack of recruits and the standards of selection remained high. Nor was their performance in action ever found wanting, as the preceding and the following pages show only too clearly. It was perhaps inevitable that the Corps, claiming such expertise in both martial duties, should, to some specialists in each, appear to fall between two

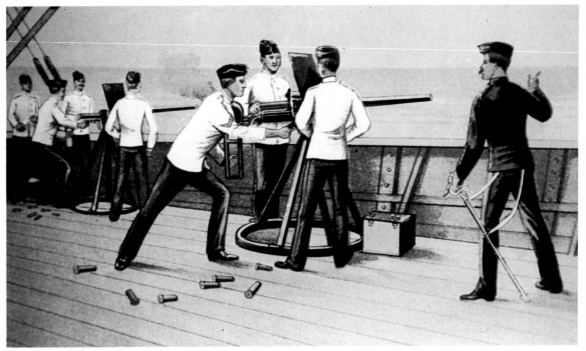

R.M.L.I. manning quick-firing guns aboard ship at the turn of
the century. (From a recruiting poster, R.M. Museum).

stools. Happily their actions and example outshone any discontentment
and the Royal Marines only added to their already established glory
during the years of Victoria and Edward.

Nor did it retard the Corps' faith in its future. Today we know that
their future lies increasingly in the air as well as on sea and land, and in
1911 Lieutenant G. Wildman Lushington and Lieutenant E.L. Gerrard
became the first Royal Marines to take to the sky, Gerrard going on to
lead the first air raid over Germany in 1914.

Service Afloat 1914/18

The Great War commenced for Great Britain on August 4th, 1914, but
two days before, at 2.30 a.m. on August 2nd, the mobilisation telegrams
had been despatched and the Royal Marines were ready on 'The Day'. The
great bulk of their forces were embarked in the heavy units of the fleets,
the battleships, battle-cruisers and cruisers, while others were allocated
to battalions of the Royal Marine Brigade and to the Royal Marine
Artillery batteries later established both at home and abroad in defence of
ports and harbours. On August 4th the serving strength of the Corps was
18,360 officers and men and, despite very heavy casualties in the
intervening period, by the time of the Armistice in 1918 it had grown to a
strength of 55,521.

While, therefore, the majority of the Corps was afloat serving with the
fleets in every theatre of war, an account of their activities would merely
read like a list of naval actions and battles of the First World War and be a
meaningless exercise. Suffice it to say then that there was not a sea battle
during the entire course of the war at which the Royal Marines were not

present. The greatest, although ultimately indecisive, battle of the whole period was of course Jutland on May 31st, 1916, when the Corps suffered very heavy casualties as a result of the loss of the battle-cruisers *Queen Mary*, *Invincible* and *Indefatigable* and the armoured cruisers *Black Prince* and *Warrior*.

The conduct of the Royal Marines afloat can perhaps best be illustrated by an act of unrivalled heroism shown at Jutland by a Major of the R.M.L.I. aboard the battle-cruiser *Lion*, flagship of Admiral Sir David Beatty. In the initial stages of the battle the two rival squadrons of mighty battle-cruisers were slugging it out. At 4 p.m. the great ships were exchanging salvoes of one-ton missiles at a range of 16,000 yards. It was then that the *Lion* was hit by a heavy shell on the roof of 'Q' turret. The roof was torn off and the shell penetrated into the gunhouse where it exploded with great carnage among the gun crew and those in the control position. Major Francis Harvey, R.M.L.I., had both legs shot off and was mortally wounded but nonetheless he managed to order the flooding of

Major F.J.W. Harvey, V.C., R.M.L.I. (From a painting by an unknown artist, R.M. Museum).

the magazine to prevent the flames from reaching it. His dying words were complied with and shortly afterwards a second explosion in the turret was caused by smouldering material setting off a charge. The flash passed down the trunk in a great sheet of flame which killed immediately all the magazine and shellroom personnel, but was halted at the closed magazine doors thus preventing the destruction of the *Lion*. For his devotion to duty and great presence of mind Major Harvey was posthumously awarded the Victoria Cross.

Another example of how this devotion to duty applied to the whole Corps from officer to the youngest recruit can be illustrated by the story of young Bugler, S.C. Reed. He was one of the 96 officers and men of the Marines aboard the old battleship *Formidable* which was torpedoed in a rising gale off West Bay in the Channel. Encountering extreme difficulties, due to the weather, it was very hard to get the men off and two officers and 84 Royal Marines were lost. The senior surviving officer later recounted how he had seen Bugler Reed, who was sixteen years old,

The battle-cruiser H.M.S. *Lion* in which Major Harvey, R.M.L.I. won his Victoria Cross at the Battle of Jutland in May, 1916. (From the painting by Arthur Burgess, Imperial War Museum).

standing on the quarterdeck after the last boats had left the sinking battleship. In reply to a question of how he was, he replied, "Alright". It was suggested that he use his drum to keep him afloat but he replied that he had already thought of this idea and had therefore given his drum to one of the young boy sailors of more tender months than himself as the boy had nothing. Reed added that he was not at all nervous as he prepared to abandon ship, but he was not among the survivors.

At the great surrender of the German High Seas Fleet to the Grand Fleet under Sir David Beatty on November 21st, 1918, almost 5,000 men of the Corps were present in the magnificent array of British warships, and for the majority of these Marines this was their first and only sight of their German opponents after over four years of war.

Those Marines that served in the air during the Great War also added lustre to the Corps and indeed the very first D.S.O. awarded to the Marines during this conflict was won by Lieutenant Collet, R.M.A., for a daring bombing attack on the Zeppelin sheds at Dusseldorf in the first month of the war.

The Defence of Antwerp

Although pre-war plans had been made for the formation of a 'Flying Column' of Royal Marines little could at first be done, but by August 25th, 1914, four battalions had been formed by the Chatham, Plymouth and Portsmouth R.M.L.I. and the R.M.A. On that day they were sent over to Ostend without any indication of their mission. They entered the line before the town on the 28th but were pulled back to England on 31st without seeing any action. On 12th September from this Royal Marines Brigade which had been formed at Walmer, Kent, 150 picked men were sent to Dunkirk as a mobile force, the 'Motor Bandits', and, with their armoured cars, carried out patrols in France and Belgium with great dash, until withdrawn. On September 19th the Marines Brigade was again sent over to Dunkirk as part of the embryo Royal Naval Division where they used London buses as transports for a while. By September 30th the two great armies, trying to outflank each other, were approaching the coast, while in Belgium the Antwerp forts had been demolished by the great Austrian siege-guns the Germans had brought up. In an attempt to hold Antwerp, Winston Churchill, the First Lord of the Admiralty, had flung in the Royal Marines Brigade to try and stave off the fall of this valuable port.

Under the command of Brigadier-General A. Paris, R.M.A. the 1st R.N. Brigade and the Marines took over the line from the exhausted Belgians on the 4th October. The shallow Belgian trenches offered no protection and were quickly improved and soon the force was in action against the advancing German troops. Under Lieutenant-Colonel C. McN. Parsons, R.M.L.I., the Marines fought hard until the 6th, when a Belgian defeat on their flank forced them to fall back. Under Colonel A.E. Marchant they were again pulled back to man Antwerp's inner defences and so missed some very heavy shelling of their former positions. Here they occupied decent trenches, with some wire and the river Scheldt aiding the defence. But again the Germans pressed forward all around, crossed the river and the Marines were again hastily pulled out, reaching Ostend on the 9th.

Unfortunately during the withdrawal many of the Portsmouth Battalion were cut off by the advancing Germans and they also lost many men when a train was ambushed on the 9th. After a brief spell at Ostend the Marines battalions were re-embarked for England where they arrived on the 12th October after the loss of over 400 men. During the next three months the Marines were brought up to strength at their depots in the south of England in readiness for their next operation with the Naval Division.

The Royal Marines return from Ostend in August, 1914. (From an original coloured newspaper of the period. R.M. Museum).

Major-General Sir A. Paris, K.C.B., R.M.A., commander of the Naval Division at Gallipoli, 1915. (From the painting by H. Donald Smith, R.M. Eastney).

The Dardanelles

Although it was obvious that the main battle-front lay in France, the entry of Turkey into the war on the side of the Central Powers gave rise to both problems and opportunities. It was felt in some quarters that the appearance of an Allied fleet off Instanbul would bring about an immediate Turkish surrender. It was also necessary to find a warm-water route to help supply the Russian army with food and ammunition and furthermore an attack on Turkey itself would take the pressure off the Suez Canal and the Balkans. An initial attack was made by the old battleships of the fleet against forts guarding the Dardanelles but this came to grief with heavy loss of battleships on the minefields in the straits. Therefore it was decided to put ashore an army to storm the flanks of the straits and allow the fleet through. Unfortunately much delay in assembling this force enabled the Turks to prepare strong positions in readiness.

During the first bombardments in February, 1915, protection for the demolition parties landed from the fleet had been provided by Brigadier-General Trotman's Marines force which consisted of the Chatham and Plymouth Battalions, and in a skirmish near Kum Kale, on the Asiatic shore, No. 3 Company of the Plymouth Battalion was in action against a Turkish battalion. Not until April was the Expeditionary Force, under Sir Ian Hamilton, ready to go into action. The Royal Marines contribution was large, consisting of the four battalions of the R.M. Brigade belonging to the Naval Division. On April 25th, 1915, Plymouth Battalion R.M.L.I. went ashore at 'Y' beach under the command of Colonel Matthews. Originally landed as a feint for 'X' beach, and told they would only be ashore for six hours, they were in fact in action for 30 hours and took heavy casualties. They were unsupported and received no orders. Colonel Matthews patrolled inland but his reports were ignored due to the disasters on the other beaches where the landing parties were killed in waves as they tried to land. Plymouth Battalion dug in and repelled several heavy counter-attacks, but 2 Company was then ordered to re-embark without Colonel Matthews' knowledge. This left 1, 3 and 4 Companies to hold for a further period without any assistance before Matthews ordered the survivors off on his own initiative.

On April 28th the Chatham and Portsmouth battalions landed to support the Australians who had taken heavy losses at Anzac and were joined later by Deal. They took over the centre of the line, and although they were composed of 'seventy-five percent recruits, twenty percent reservists and five percent active service', and had little or no opportunity for training since their enlistment, they held their positions ashore for fourteen days instead of the 48 hours they were told to expect.

These raw young recruits upheld the honour of the Corps for they bore the brunt of Kemal's third great attack launched to drive the British force back into the sea from their tiny footholds. Wave after wave of Turkish infantry formed up in the gullies a few hundred yards from the Royal Marines in their shallow trenches, and then flung themselves forward. Time after time they were beaten back but each time the ranks of the R.M.L.I. grew thinner. One platoon held an isolated trench for four days and three nights under such attack, and no food, water or ammunition could be got through to them. Little wonder then the R.M.L.I. wasted away.

It was at this stage that the Victoria Cross was won by Lance-Corporal W.R. Parker, R.M.L.I., who was a stretcher-bearer. He had to take supplies to a trench which was isolated by 400 yards of open ground constantly swept by machine-gun and rifle fire. Parker went forward and got through although his companion water carriers were wiped out. He managed to assist the wounded in the trench and, when the trench was evacuated, helped them back to safety.

Hereafter this campaign settled down to the same kind of stalemate as the Western Front and all through the summer Turkish and British troops faced each other under the shadow of Achi Baba, the dominating heights. Fruitless frontal attacks against barbed wire and machine-guns did nothing to ease the situation but only reduced the ranks of the R.M.L.I. still further. In the winter they were beset by blizzards which brought flooding and frostbite. Bowing to the inevitable, the troops were gradually withdrawn, General Paris and the 2nd Battalion acting as a rearguard, taken off on the 9th January, 1916. Royal Marines were thus 'First in, last out' in this tragic campaign.

Between January and May, 1916, now as the 1st and 2nd Battalions, the R.M.L.I. were with the 2nd R.N. Brigade in Salonika before sailing home to join in the great offensive on the Western Front, the Battle of the Somme.

Major F.W. Lumsden, R.M.A., awarded the Victoria Cross on the Western Front and later killed in action there. (From the painting by A. Durrant Smyth, R.M. Eastney).

In the Trenches

Once the R.M.L.I. had arrived in France some re-organisation took place. This was necessary to enable the Royal Naval Division to take its place in the line with the 'New Armies' of Kitchener and the remnants of the old regular regiments which had been decimated in the fruitless fighting of the previous two years. So the War Office took responsibility for recruiting, training, maintenance and discipline, while the Admiralty kept the duties of pay, officer appointments and the like. This did not affect the recruitment of the R.M.L.I. intake however which continued to be based at Deal, while the composition of the Royal Naval Division remained the same, with naval ranks and ratings being retained. On July 20th, 1916, the Division became the 63rd (Naval) Division and machine-gun companies were added to each of the Brigades. The Division was now sent to the trenches during a 'quiet period' to prepare itself for the battles ahead.

Just what the phrase 'quiet period' meant can be illustrated by the fate of a patrol taken over the top on the night of the 13th July, 1916, by Lieutenant W.C.A. Elliott. He was wounded and for two days and nights Private L.J. Elliott, R.M.L.I., tried to get him back to British lines but he eventually died. Private Elliot was out in 'no-man's' land for four days without food before he managed to return.

In October, well after the great Somme offensive had collapsed into a dour struggle in the mud without a breakthrough but with appalling casualties, (60,000 on the first day alone), the Division was moved into the battle zone. On October 13th, while out on a reconnaissance, General Paris was wounded badly. He was much missed for his replacement was not attuned to the special naval outlook of his command. The Division went over the top at 5.45 a.m. on November 13th, 1916, the so-called Battle of the Ancre, when their objectives included the redoubt of Beaumont Hamel in an attack against Beaucourt. Four lines of German trenches faced them, the nearest some 200 yards distant. They assaulted in four waves and, within seven minutes, they had all attacked in the face of a heavy German barrage and intense machine-gun fire. They succeeded in gaining the third enemy trench but at enormous cost. When the survivors arrived there they found little to show for their efforts.

Sergeant Meatyard later wrote: 'The German trench we were now in was in a chronic state, once you took a step you had a job to get your leg out, the mud being so deep and sticky. Wounded Germans and our own men were lying about all over the place; what had been dug-outs were now partly closed by the muddy landslides that had taken place, as the result of our gun fire, and choked the entrances'.

Under the leadership of Colonel Freyberg the attacks were continued for thirty hours. At the end of it they had taken a few more yards of muddy trenches. The 1st Battalion, R.M.L.I., went over the top with 400 men and were reinforced often during the two days fighting. They were withdrawn on the 15th, 138 strong.

After further periods of rest in and out of the line the Marines saw further examples of this type of warfare, being present at the Battles of Miraumont (17/18th February, 1917), Gavrelle (23/24th April, 1917) and Arleux (28/29th April, 1917). Their losses were constant and their ranks continued to dwindle. The most severe test that the Corps had to face on the Western Front was at the Battle of Passchendaele between 26th October and 10th November, 1917.

Their objective was the line of the Paddebeek Brook and the troops attacked at 5.40 a.m. on October 26th. The ground was terrible for it had rained all the previous night and it continued to do so throughout the 26th. The 1st Battalion R.M.L.I., led by Lieutenant-Colonel Ozanee, attacked in three lines into the swamp of mud and water to advance to lines of enemy trenches, which, although marked on maps with great clarity, were in effect little more than undulations and shell holes amidst the mire. Lieutenant P. Ligertwood took 'A' Company across the line of the Paddebeek and, although he was wounded three times, held his position. Wounded a fourth time he told his men to continue forward before he died. After fierce fighting, the 2nd Battalion was forced back across the brook but a front line was finally stabilised some 350 yards further on from the start positions. The 1/R.M.L.I. took more than 280 casualties and the 2/R.M.L.I. almost 400 to achieve this gain.

General Gough sent the message, '. . . no troops could have had to face worse conditions of mud', and continued, 'No troops could have done more than our men did today'.

Further fighting followed on Welch Ridge in the Cambrai salient when a heavy attack was made by the Germans across the snow which penetrated the Corps positions which were lightly held, especially those of the 1/R.M.L.I., but they gave no ground. Fighting continued the next day and the Germans finally gained the high ground before the battle petered out. By 1918 the Royal Marines in France were reduced to two battalions and these took the brunt of the great German offensive which began on March 21st, 1918. Being forced back after attacks with storm troops and mustard gas the Naval Brigade fought as a rearguard during the retreat and then on April 6th they counter-attacked against Aveluy Wood.

After the casualties received during this period of intensive fighting the two surviving R.M.L.I. Battalions had not enough reserves to make up their numbers and were amalgamated as the First Battalion, R.M.L.I. for the last six months of the war. Under the command of Colonel E.K. Fletcher this battalion took part in the victorious battles that marked the Allied counter-offensive and which only ended with the Armistice in November, 1918. The 1/R.M.L.I. thus fought at the Battle of Albert (21/23rd August) during which Colonel Fletcher was both gassed and wounded. He died in 1922 at Deal Barracks. At the beginning of September the battalion forced the junction of the Drocourt/Queant Switch and Hindenburg lines and crossed the Canal du Nord at the end of the month. They fought at the Second Battle of Cambrai and the Armistice found the Battalion near the Belgian village of Villiers St. Ghislain near Mons. As Winston Churchill would later write of the part they played on the Western Front; 'Their reputation was consistently maintained in spite of losses of so awful a character as to sweep away, three or four times over, the original personnel'.

In June, 1919, before disbanding, they were reviewed by H.R.H. the Prince of Wales who said, 'There are few here today of those to whom the King bade farewell in February, 1915'. One of these few was Captain T.H. Burton, M.C., Quartermaster of the Deal Battalion, but over 6,000 of his comrades did not come back, the Corps greatest losses ever.

The Big Guns

After the operations at Ostend in 1914 a recommendation was put forward that the R.M.A. should form three field artillery brigades and one howitzer brigade to work with the Naval Division but this was not done and a Howitzer brigade and an Anti-aircraft brigade were formed instead. The Howitzer Brigade, R.M.A. was formed to man the 15-inch howitzers designed by the Coventry Ordnance Works in reply to the big Austrian guns which had smashed the Belgian fortresses. Admiral Bacon was manager of these works and he was re-commissioned as a Colonel in the R.M.A. to enable him to take the guns into action.

Each of these huge weapons fired a 1,400 lb shell some 10,800 yards. The range was short for so large a projectile and the hazards of utilising such enormous guns close to the front had to be accepted. Twelve of these guns were ordered by the Admiralty, of which eleven saw service on the Western Front. They could be broken down for transport and each howitzer had a train of eleven tractors and twelve trucks and a total of 88 men per gun to operate them. The first of them went into action at Locre on March 6th, 1915, and thereafter they were used in support of almost every major assault. All ten then in service fired in support of the Somme offensive but they operated as single guns rather than as a composite brigade. Two of the guns were lost during the retreat of 1918, after their breeches had been saved, while a premature explosion in another the same year wrote it off. Although others suffered hits during their 3½ years service, none were destroyed.

In April, 1915, Admiral Bacon was succeeded by Major F.W. Lumsden, R.M.A., who served until July before going to the First Army. While commanding the 17th Highland Light Infantry this gallant officer won the Corps' third Victoria Cross of the war when he led artillery teams through intense enemy fire to bring in six captured German guns. This outstanding officer also won three bars to his D.S.O. before being killed on June 3rd, 1918, in the trenches.

The Anti-Aircraft brigade was formed at Eastney in December, 1914, and was a novel and specialised form of gunnery of which little was then known of its capabilities or limitations. The 2-pdr pompom was adopted by Colonel Osmaston and mounted on special armoured lorries each with support lorries containing personnel, ammunition and the like. The pompoms had special sights and the brigade crossed to France in April, 1915, with a total strength of 280 officers and men. On the 30th, 'B' battery, in action near Coudekerque, claimed to have brought down its first aircraft. The brigade worked close behind the lines and provided effective covering fire for trenches, airfields and artillery positions at Ypres, Dunkirk, Nieuport and elsewhere during the continued Flanders fighting. Some lorries were destroyed by shells as soon as they revealed themselves, others had their crews caught in mustard-gas attacks but nonetheless the brigade doubled in size by 1916 and was in great demand. During the latter years of the war the increased height attained by the newer German aircraft brought about the re-arming of the brigade with the 3-inch gun. Batteries commanded by Major Briscoe and Major Cartwright continued in action until the Armistice and were finally disbanded on January 16th, 1919, at Eastney.

When they captured Ostend in 1914 the Germans protected their lines near the sea from bombardment by ships of the Royal Navy by mounting the *Tirpitz* battery of 11-inch guns to keep them at bay. As a counter threat to these guns, and in repeated efforts to destroy the lock gates of Zeebrugge and Ostend by shell fire, Admiral Bacon had mounted a single 12-inch and four 9.2-inch naval guns at Dunkirk. In December, 1915, Captain H. Peck, R.M.A., arrived for duties as adjutant with these guns.

The 12-inch gun, named *Dominion*, was mounted inside a dummy barn at Adinkerke, and the 9.2-inch guns at Groenendijk, one of them, named *Eastney*, being manned by the R.M.A. under Captain J.H. Hollingsworth. To support the Passchendaele offensive in 1917 two more 12-inch and several 9.2-inch guns were added to this unit and the R.M.A. took over all these weapons to form the R.M.A. Siege Train, with 500 men and seventeen guns including six 7.5-inch.

Between June 1917, and the end of the war the three British 12-inch guns duelled with a long-range German gun, a 15-inch weapon called *Leugenboom*, but neither side was ever put out of action. The British guns had extreme ranges of up to 30,000 yards, and in March, 1918, carried out a shoot at 32,000 yards. After the Armistice the guns were dismantled and the unit returned to England, being disbanded at Eastney in March, 1919.

Other R.M.A. artillery units served ashore, guarding bases like Scapa Flow, while others served in the field in South-West and East Africa, and trained the South African heavy artillery units.

Zeebrugge

The desperate situation at sea, where German submarines had been sinking enormous numbers of Allied merchant vessels, had been one of the reasons for the ghastly land offensive of 1917, the Navy hoping that the Army would clear the coast and take the ports of Ostend and Zeebrugge which served as advance bases for the U-boats. When this failed, the convoy system was introduced and helped the situation but meanwhile Admiral Keyes had been most pressing in his determination to block these ports and the Zeebrugge operation was therefore put into effect on the night of the 23rd April, 1918. The plan was for three obsolete cruisers to be sunk in the canal mouth but, as the approaches were guarded by a long concrete mole bristling with guns, another old cruiser, the *Vindictive*, was specially converted to take the Royal Marines, and a Naval storming party, alongside to take or silence the guns.

The 4th Battalion, Royal Marines, had been raised in 1917 to go to Ireland after the rebellion there in 1916 but this move had been cancelled and the battalion was disbanding when, in January, 1918, they reformed at Deal with three full-strength R.M.L.I. companies. Here they were inspected by King George V in March. Meanwhile R.M.A. volunteers formed a

Trench Mortar Section to give covering fire from the *Vindictive*. The whole force was under the command of Lieutenant-Colonel B.N. Elliot and the Marine storming party was to be led by 'C' Company under Major B.G. Weller, D.S.O., who had won the honour of first ashore by drawing lots. To enable them to storm the mole, which was considerably higher than the *Vindictive's* deck, fourteen narrow 'brows' had been rigged so that they could be dropped into position on the outer wall.

The approach was made in drizzle and under cover of an elaborate smoke screen laid by the escorting destroyers, but, at the last moment, the wind whipped this cover away and the *Vindictive* was subjected to a deluge of shot and shell which swept her decks and upperworks killing and wounding large numbers of the assembled storming party, including Elliot and Captain Halahan, R.N., on the bridge. Command was assumed by Major Weller and the attack proceeded although all but two of the brows had been destroyed and the *Vindictive* had berthed outside the fortified area of the mole. Further complications were added by the fact that two German destroyers were berthed inside the mole and they began to shoot at the upperworks of the *Vindictive* with their guns. Fire was particularly concentrated on the foretop gun position which was giving valuable covering fire and shells smashed into this killing every man there save two and these were both wounded. Sergeant N.A. Finch, R.M.A., was one of these but he continued to work the gun. For this he was awarded the Victoria Cross by ballot.

Meanwhile the pitiful remains of the storming parties managed to get ashore through a hail of machine-gun fire and, led by Captain E. Bamford, D.S.O., the Portsmouth Company fought their way along the sea wall while the Plymouth Company, under Lieutenant C.R.W. Lamplough, lowered themselves on to the mole and took one of the sheds which they formed into a strong-point before attacking towards the head of the mole.

The gun batteries were assaulted by the seamen storming party with great gallantry but heavy loss and No. 12 platoon of Marines, under Lieutenant G. Underhill, was sent to their assistance. Meanwhile disembarkation continued with ladders, at the foot of which, it was reported, lay a pile of German dead who had tried to knock them away.

Meanwhile Captain Bamford and his party continued to advance in the face of severe fire. As was later recorded; 'When on the mole and under heavy fire he displayed the greatest initiative in the command of his company and by his total disregard of danger showed a magnificent example to his men. He first established a strong point on the right of the disembarkation, and when satisfied that that was safe, led an assault on a battery to the left with the utmost coolness and valour'.

When the recall sounded the storming parties re-embarked taking their wounded with them. Captain Bamford later received the Victoria Cross,

The Royal Marines landing from the *Vindictive* at Zeebrugge, 1918. (From the painting by de Lacey, The Depot, R.M. Deal).

also after a ballot. But the Marines left behind them on the mole many of the 353 dead out of the 700 men involved. Alas for their gallantry, the blocking operation was not a complete success. But in honour of the outstanding conduct of the Battalion it was decided that no other unit should ever again bear the title of the 4th Battalion, Royal Marines, thus preserving their glory in the name itself.

It was during his visit to the 4th Battalion at Deal barracks that His Majesty King George V directed that the Senior Squad should in future, be known as the 'King's Squad' and that the best all-round recruit would wear the Royal Cypher as 'King's Badgeman'. This practice continues today and the design still consists of King George V's cypher.

Fighting the Bolsheviks

In addition to the main battle fronts on land and at sea, the Royal Marines served during the Great War in many other roles and took part in a large number of lesser campaigns. Detachments fought in Egypt, Mesopotamia, the Persian Gulf and the Red Sea against the Turks, finally completing their contribution to the downfall of this enemy by taking part in the Palestine campaign and, during the Turkish peace negotiations, the occupation of the Gallipoli forts in 1918. The Marines also saw service and some fighting in Greece, South-West Africa and East Africa, suppressed a mutiny in Singapore, stood, 45 strong, between two rival armies, the

Rumanian and the Hungarian, on the bridges of Budapest, and took part in the occupation of the German Cameroons while the 8th Battalion was stationed in Ireland between 1916 and 1922.

After the Armistice with Germany, however, two loose ends remained to be cleared up. The first was the Turkish question, which dragged on for more years than the war itself, and the second was the problem of the Bolshevik uprising in Russia and the subsequent decision of the British Government to intervene in a limited manner on the side of the 'White' Russian forces in their battles against the 'Red' Russian armies. The Royal Marines who were caught up in this complicated struggle found themselves fighting with Allies of a dubious nature in the vast wilderness of Siberia and up in the Arctic Circle at Murmansk, while others were involved at Sebastopol in the Crimea and other Black Sea ports.

The old battleship *Glory* had been stationed at Murmansk in 1917 and was reinforced by the armoured cruiser *Cochrane* in March, 1918. Their Marines saw action on the Norwegian frontier against the 'White' Finns,

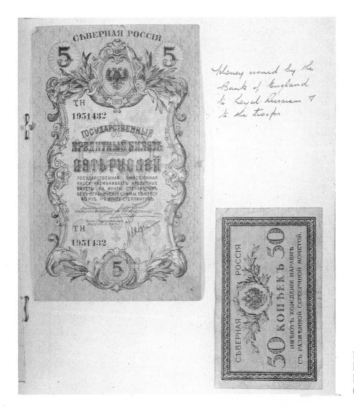

Russia, 1919. The Diary of Captain W.D. Craig, R.M.A., who served in the Royal Marines Field Force. Special currency was issued at this time. (R.M. Museum).

pro-German troops, during May, 1918. The problem was how to preserve Murmansk from the 'Red' Army and, in July, a Royal Marines Field Force arrived as reinforcements. They also formed a ski column from the R.M.L.I. which fought the Red Army. Some American seamen and French troops were also based there at this time.

On May 3rd, 1919, a company consisting of elements of the R.M.A., Chatham, Portsmouth, Plymouth and Lewis Gun platoons, under Colonel Lecky of the Army, went into action with some French infantry and White Russians at Urozeroy. The following day they fought off attacks by an armoured train and took Maselskaya.

In the August of 1919 the 6th R.M. Battalion under Lieutenant-Colonel A. de W. Kitcat, R.M.L.I., arrived at Murmansk and went into action near Lake Onega, 300 miles south of Kem. This was not a happy period and some men refused duties and at a subsequent court martial thirteen received the death sentence and others five years penal servitude, although the sentences were reduced in most cases. In an attack at

The family tradition of the Corps is well illustrated here with this fine case of medals won by three generations of the Reynolds family. (R.M. Museum).

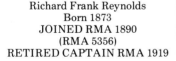

Richard Frank Reynolds
Born 1873
JOINED RMA 1890
(RMA 5356)
RETIRED CAPTAIN RMA 1919

Herbert James Reynolds
Born 1898
JOINED RMA 1915
(RMA 14760)
DISCHARGE BY PURCHASE 1921

Frank Reynolds
Born 1928
JOINED ROYAL MARINES 1945
PLY/X114836)
COMMISSIONED 1946
RETIRED MAJOR RM 1971

Ussuna under Major Ridings, R.M.A., H.Q. company was fired upon by 'D' Company and then both ran into a system of trenches which they were unable to take. A similar attack on Koikori by 'B' and 'C' Companies, under Major Williams of the Army, was ambushed and cut up. The British Force was finally withdrawn in September.

Another small force of R.M.L.I. and R.M.A. operated in the Caspian Sea area as part of 'Dunster' force in 1918 on the Persian frontier, at the Baku oilfields and in the Causacus. 160 Marines garrisoned Petovsk with two 6-inch guns from Mudros. Between April and June, 1919, a Royal Marine detachment landed by the cruisers *Kent* and *Suffolk*, under Captain T.H. Jameson, fought against the Red Armies on the Kama river with a 6-inch gun and four 12-pounders and a series of small gunboats. Deep in the heart of Siberia their only link with the outside world was the Trans-Siberian railway to Vladivostock, while another party under Captain Bath fought on the Volga front.

Finally the 11th Battalion went out to Turkey in October, 1922 for a year during the Chanak incident when Kemal Ataturk's forces threatened the British occupation force there. This problem was finally settled with the Treaty of Lausanne in 1923.

Between the Wars

Following the end of the 'War to end all wars' there was naturally a period of strong retrenchment. During the Great War the Royal Marines, including such diverse units as the R.M. Engineers, the R.M. Labour Corps and the R.M. Submarine Miners, formed to carry out specialist tasks, had reached a strength of some 55,000 men but by 1919 the Corps was down to a strength of 15,000. Following the Washington Naval Conference of 1922, the Royal Navy was reduced from the largest fleet in the world to a quarter of its former size to bring it down on a par with the United States of America. Wholesale scrapping of warships took place and a correspondingly large reduction in the Royal Marines establishment was called for, the Treasury even going so far as to demand its abolition.

Fortunately there were a few men of vision who were not impressed by the ability of the League of Nations to do more than pass desirable motions which it could not enforce, but nonetheless the Corps, although retained, was cut further to a strength of 9,500, which meant the abolition of one division.

In 1923 the decision was made to amalgamate the two branches of the Royal Marines, the R.M.A and the R.M.L.I. They became once more the Royal Marines and the old Forton Barracks were closed down at Gosport, leaving Eastney to become the Portsmouth Division. His Majesty King

George V sent the following message to the Corps. 'As their Colonel-in-Chief, I desire to express to them my appreciation of their former services, and I am confident that, under the new title of Royal Marines, they will continue to maintain that reputation for loyalty and devotion to duty which has ever been the pride of the Corps of Royal Marines'.

Again it became the prime function of the Marines to man the guns of the fleet and all their vast experience of land and combined operations was cast aside due to financial restrictions, despite the Madden Committee of 1924 having recommended that a brigade of 3,000 men should be based ashore and a mobile base defence organization set up.

Royal Marine Police were formed in 1922 from R.M. Pensioners to ensure the security of the Dockyards and in 1924 Royal Marines officers were allowed to join the Fleet Air Arm, then under Royal Air Force control, and many did so.

It was not long, however, before the infantry qualities of the Royal Marines, coupled with their state of instant readiness, were called upon for a

Royal Marines on Guard Duty at St. James's in 1935. (From the painting by Gerald Hudson, The Depot, R.M. Deal).

land operation of the type for which they were famed. The Chinese Nationalist Armies were advancing upon Shanghai and, as usual, there was an incredible amount of confused fighting in China between armies and irregular bands. As always in such cases, the safety of European civilians was gravely endangered and in 1927 the 12th Battalion, Royal Marines, was formed at Eastney with a company from each division and shipped out on January 25th. They served as a peaceful influence at Shanghai for a year, as part of the Defence Force until the area calmed down, before returning home and disbanding.

The mutinies in the Atlantic Fleet, in October, 1931, were brought about by a drastic cut in the pay of the seamen and the indifferent way in which, as so many times in the past, the Government handled the situation. As in 1797, the overwhelming majority of the Royal Marines remained loyal.

August, 1935, saw the Royal Marines assuming ceremonial duties in London. They mounted guard at Buckingham Palace and St. James's Palace and on completion of their tour of duty they exercised their old right to march through the City with due ceremony. It was particularly appropriate that 1935 was chosen for this honour for it was the Silver Jubilee of King George V, the Colonel-in-Chief of the Corps.

The rise of the dictatorships in Italy, Germany and Spain, coupled with the invasion of China by Japan and the annexation of Ethiopia by Mussolini, showed just how far the League of Nations had failed and, with the withering of confidence in 'Collective Security', we belatedly looked at our own defences and found them sadly lacking.

The outbreak of World War II thus found the Royal Marines at low strength and even after the mobilization of the reserves and pensioners their numbers were raised to only 12,500 men and the bulk of them went to the ships of the Fleet.

Action at Sea and in the Air, 1939/45

As in the Great War, the Royal Marines served extensively in the ships of the Royal Navy right through the war and no action, be it Malta Convoy or the destruction of German heavy ships, took place without the help of Royal Marines gun crews. Serving in the big ships, the battleships and cruisers, in the traditional Marines gun turret, 'X' mounting, (this was usually the super-imposed mounting aft), they fired their huge shells at the *Graf Spee*, the *Bismark* and the *Scharnhorst*, while at the end of the war they directed their 14-inch projectiles against Japanese factories close to Tokyo. At Matapan and Spartivento they fought ships of the Italian navy. Royal Marines Pensioners served afloat in defensively equipped merchant ships and manned a host of weapons on all manner of vessels.

In the air, the Royal Marines also played their part and participated in the first and also in one of the last aircraft operations. On September 14th, 1939, Lieutenant G.B.K. Griffiths, R.M., flying a Swordfish aircraft from the aircraft carrier *Ark Royal*, carried out an attack against the German submarine *U. 30*, but was brought down by the blast of his own explosion and made prisoner. One decoration won by the Corps early in World War II was in fact awarded to Captain R.T. Partridge the pilot of a Skua dive-bomber over Norway in April, 1940.

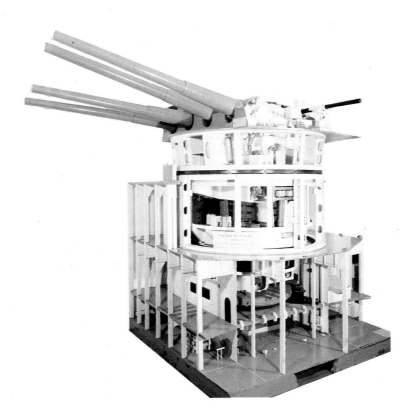

A cut-away model of a battleship's 14-inch gun turret. (R.M. Museum).

Forced to land after damaging a Heinkel 111 he subsequently made the German aircrew P.O.W.'s although his own crew were themselves unarmed. For his 'daring and resource' on this occasion Partridge received the D.S.O. Between June and November, 1942, Major A.C. Newson, R.M., commanded a squadron of Albacore bombers which helped the Eighth Army in the Western Desert, and as better aircraft became available to the Navy from America so the Royal Marines pilots were able to do more with them.

In the great carrier attacks upon the oil refineries in Japanese-held Sumatra in 1944, Captain Ronnie Hay, R.M., was the Flight Co-Ordinator for the mass attacks by Avenger bombers and Corsair fighters which caused great destruction. There were a number of Royal Marines in the British Pacific Fleet aircraft which attacked targets ashore during the battle of Okinawa and helped finish off the Japanese Navy by bomb and rocket strikes against them in the Inland Sea in July, 1945.

A typical example of their devoted work can be illustrated by the exploits of Captain V.B.G. Cheesman, R.M., of the *Albatross*. He piloted a Walrus amphibian off the West African coast and went to the aid of a torpedoed merchant vessel. 'For hours he taxied to and fro, encouraging the men in the water, formed them into groups for greater ease of rescue, and actually towed some of the ship's boats to within their reach.' He was awarded the M.B.E.

Norway

On April 9th, 1940, German forces invaded neutral Norway and quickly took control of the southern part of the country. In an attempt to redress this situation the Allies landed hastily assembled troops in central and northern Norway, but, being without air cover and lacking heavy equipment, they were soon hard pressed. In this campaign, as in so many others, the Royal Marines were 'first in, last out' again. On April 14th the Marines of the cruisers *Sheffield* and *Glasgow* were put ashore at Namsos under Major W.F. Edds, R.M. to cover the landing of troops.

Led by Lieutenant-Colonel H.W. Simpson, R.M. another Marines force, known by the unwarlike name of 'Force Primrose' and consisting of Marines from the battleships *Nelson*, *Barham* and *Hood* which were in dock in England at the time, were put ashore at Andalsnes to cover a thrust from the south towards Trondheim. By the 29th they had been withdrawn.

At Namsos a 3.7-inch howitzer battery delayed the British destroyers waiting to evacuate them until every man and gun were aboard.

Captain G.W. Wilson, R.M. explained to the Navy, 'It is not the policy of the Corps to leave its equipment in enemy hands'.

Another Marine exploit during this unhappy campaign was the landing of a detachment under Major G.V. Walton, R.M. from the battleship *Resolution* at Ae Fiord. Whilst operating in this area of the Narvik, or northern front, they skilfully rescued some British seamen from two trawlers who had been captured by German paratroops.

At the beginning of the war a special Gun Mounting Party of Marines had been withdrawn from duties on the East Coast and formed into the Royal Marines Fortress Unit under Lieutenant-Colonel H.R. Lambert, R.M. This unit supervised the offloading of guns and mountings in the Narvik area until its base ship was sunk and Lambert was wounded. It was withdrawn on May 26th and formed the nucleus of M.N.B.D.O.2 back in England. The last troops off were a party of Marines under Captain H.G. Hasler, R.M., whom we shall meet later.

What Women? When the 'Marens' re-joined the Corps early in the war they were not always *recognised* by stern traditionalists! (From the cartoon by Hynes, R.M. Museum).

Following the German invasion of Denmark, both the Faroes and Iceland were occupied by Marines, the former on the 13th May by 200 Marines under Lieutenant-Colonel T.B.W. Sandall, R.M. embarked in the cruiser *Suffolk*, and the latter, on the 10th May, by a force consisting of the 2nd Battalion, Royal Marines, under Colonel R.G. Sturgess, R.M., with a 4-inch and a 2-pdr battery from M.N.B.D.O.1 and a Naval Howitzer battery. These forces were both relieved by the army later in the year and operated without loss.

Backs to the Wall

The main German attacks, which resulted in the fall of Holland, Belgium and France, and the evacuation of the B.E.F., began on May 10th, 1940. The following day a special force of 200 men, which included a King's Squad, under Major B.G.B. Mitchell, R.M., was formed at Chatham Barracks and transported to the Hook of Holland. Between 12th and 15th May they acted as a rearguard while the Dutch Royal Family was got away. Another force of 100 Marines, led by Major C.F.L. Holford R.M., was taken to Boulogne in a similar way and covered the demolition parties there, pulling out next day. Finally yet a third Marine force, 85 strong, under Captain G.W.A. Courtice, R.M., went to Calais but almost all were either killed or captured upon the fall of the port.

Britain was now alone and preparations were made for defence against invasion. The R.M. Gun-Mounting Unit had already installed 133 guns, from 6-inch downward, on the south-east coast but, with the Germans across the Channel, a R.M. Siege Regiment was formed at Dover. They manned two 15-inch guns, named *Winnie* and *Pooh*, for convoy protection and cross-channel duelling, and further heavy guns were added later. During the Battle of Britain, in the autumn of 1940, the 1st R.M. Heavy A.A. Regiment claimed a total of 98 enemy aircraft destroyed, a record.

A Royal Marines Division, three brigades strong, was authorised. The first two brigades, the 101st and 102nd, went to West Africa for the abortive Dakar operation in August, 1940, while the 103rd was forming at Lympstone. In February, 1941, M.N.B.D.O.1 sailed to the Mediterranean and set up a base at Suda Bay, Crete. When the German paratroops overran the island in May, 1941, the Marines lost some 1,200 men of the 2,000 on the island. The one bright spot was when Major R. Garrett, R.M. refloated a disabled landing craft, and, using sacks for sails, reached North Africa after an eight-day voyage with 139 volunteers aboard. For

Major R. Garrett, R.M., escaping with his party from Crete in a landing craft with sacks rigged up as sails, May, 1941. (From the painting by Rowland Langmaid, R.M. Poole).

this exploit Garrett was awarded the D.S.O. An official account of this voyage stated: 'Two of the marines improvised a distilling plant consisting of petrol tins connected by a rubber tube, and, by using the fuel which had failed in the engines, produced 4½ gallons of drinkable water in two days. Although two of the company died on the eighth day, the ingenuity of these marines probably saved the lives of their remaining comrades'.

In September, 1941, Force 'Shortcut', from M.N.B.D.O.1 under Colonel W.B.F. Lukis, R.M. and Lieutenant-Colonel L.O. Jones, R.M., set up bases in the Indian Ocean in the Maldive Islands and the Seychelles.

The 'Plymouth Argylls' and Force 'Viper'

With the war going badly for Britain throughout 1941, the introduction of the powerful Japanese fleet and army into south-east Asia in December presented almost insurmountable problems for the British defenders of that area. Starved of tanks, fighters and the other modern weaponry, the Malayan, Burmese and even some Indian outposts fell easy prey once the Japanese were ashore. Only the bare nucleus of a British fleet, the *Prince of Wales* and *Repulse* with four destroyers, could be despatched. Shortage of aircraft carriers meant that they had no air cover and, when located by two squadrons of Japanese torpedo bombers and a squadron of heavy

The Argyll Bowl. The Royal Marines Rugby Trophy which commemorates the 'Plymouth Argylls' at Singapore, 1941-42. (45 Commando, R.M.).

bombers, both capital ships were very quickly sunk. The Japanese invasion then proceeded without further serious hindrance from the sea.

The Royal Marines detachments from both these capital ships, some 300 in all, were rescued and taken back to Singapore. Some went into hospital while others were re-kitted at the Naval Barracks and re-formed under Captain R.G.S. Lang, R.M. from the *Repulse*. A smaller party, under Captain C.D.L. Aylwin, R.M. from the *Prince of Wales*, was sent to guard the Kranji wireless station while a third party, led by Lieutenant R.J.L. Davis, R.M. had a crash course in jungle warfare and was sent up country to engage the Japanese who were now pressing down towards Singapore island.

This third group reached Port Swettenham and became attached to an Army unit during the five day withdrawal that followed, being bombed and machine-gunned all the way back. The 2nd Battalion Argyll and Sutherland Highlanders, under Lieutenant-Colonel I.M. Stewart, D.S.O. were the last British troops across the causeway, their strength reduced to 250 men during the long retreat. The Royal Marines were therefore sent to join them to make up a composite battalion. Because their two ships had been Plymouth based vessels it was inevitable that the battalion became known as the 'Plymouth Argylls'. When the Japanese attacked the island on February 9th, 1942, the battalion fought at Bukit Timah. Marine R.W. Steddon recalled an incident when they became surrounded. 'Colonel Stewart cried, "Come on, Marines", and we charged forward with our Bren guns. The japs wore all sorts of rigs. Some were in shorts, some with equipment, others without; some wore only sarongs. You couldn't tell whether they were Japs or Malays or Chinese. The undergrowth was very dense, and we had to open up at random. I was doing a bit of spraying with my tommy gun and got some of them'.

Despite much hard fighting, Singapore was overrun and very few of the battalion survived. The Japanese pressed on with equal speed into Burma, the British forces there also falling back towards the Indian border. Another Royal Marines party, Major D. Johnson, R.M. and some 106 men from M.N.B.D.O.1, was sent up the Irrawaddy river in launches. Known as Force 'Viper', this little flotilla arrived at Rangoon on the 11th and, after helping with the destruction of the vast oil refineries there, acted as a floating rearguard for the retreating army. On the 17th March they were attacked at Henzada and were ambushed again on the 27th at Padaung. Not until May 15th did they reach Tonhe, only 48 strong, to march into India and safety.

The Royal Marines Commandos & other special units

At home, the Royal Marines Division was held ready, but was never used. The Seige Regiment had been reinforced by naval guns on rail mountings known as *Peacemaker* and *Sceneshifter*. Royal Marines also served as gunners on the anti-aircraft forts in the Thames estuary. The Royal Marines Engineers were revived.

Royal Marines had continued to operate in limited combined operations roles during 1942 and 1943. An example of the Royal Marines work is afforded by the occupation of Madagascar in May, 1942. This was a pre-emptive operation to take the island from the Vichy French before they could be 'persuaded' to allow the Japanese to use it, as had happended in Indo-China. An Army force commanded by Major-General Sturgess, Commander of the Royal Marines Division, was landed, covered by a large fleet. Diego Suarez quickly fell but the narrow approaches to the vital port of Antsirane were strongly held. A party of Royal Marines, 50 strong, from the *Ramillies*, under Captain Martin Price, R.M., was taken in by the destroyer *Anthony*, which was skilfully handled. While the main attack was mounted against the two forts, the *Anthony* slipped in astern to land the Marines. They disembarked at the mole and, under cover of the destroyer's guns, advanced inland. 'As we left the wharf', recalled Captain Martin Price, 'fire was opened upon us, but they were obviously firing at the patter of little feet, which seemed to have grown several sizes larger than usual and to be scooping up all the tin cans and pebbles in the neighbourhood. As soon as we were clear, the nuisance stopped'. All the objectives were quickly taken and the surprised Vichy fortress fell. The Marines were re-embarked aboard the battleship *Ramillies* where they were greeted by the cry, 'Good lads, good old Marines!'.

It was not until 1942 that the first Royal Marines Commando was formed, being joined soon after by a second. Known initially as 'A' and 'B' Commandos, they later became 40 and 41 and, in August, 1942 the first of these had its baptism of fire at Dieppe, which was a great failure, with heavy losses. When the Canadians were pinned down on the beach, the Royal Marines Commando was sent in to reinforce them but this proved impossible. They were only saved from enormous losses by the bravery of Lieutenant-Colonel J. Picton-Phillipps, R.M., who, before he was killed, donned white gloves and stood fully exposed to wave away the oncoming landing craft containing his men.

On the night of September 13-14th, 1942 the 11th R.M. Battalion mounted a raid against Tobruk behind Rommel's lines in the desert. This was another failure and all save 100 Marines failed to reach the shore in their makeshift landing craft, while the escorting destroyers *Sikh* and *Zulu* were sunk, as was a cruiser sent to help from Alexandria. The Marines who reached the beach were all rounded up that night and taken prisoner.

More successful was a daring raid on Bordeaux by Royal Marines canoeists. Led by Major 'Blondie' Hasler, R.M., five two-man canoes, known as 'cockles', were landed by submarine at the mouth of the Gironde to attack German merchant shipping with limpet mines. Two of the cockles got through and disabled four ships, but only Major Hasler and Marine Sparks survived to return to England. A film was later made of this exploit, 'Cockleshell Heroes'.

Meanwhile the remainder of M.N.B.D.O.1 now under Major-General W.B.F. Lukis, R.M., had moved to the east, and the whole divided up into two M.N.B. brigades. One of these commenced training for combined operations in the Arakan which never materialised. M.N.B.D.O.2 had moved to the Middle East and by July, 1943, was ready to take part in the invasion of Sicily.

A Thompson sub-machine gun as issued to Royal Marines Commandos. (R.M. Museum).

The Royal Marines had been fortunate in having their own W.R.N.S., with the Royal Marines flash and regimental badge, attached to shore units. They were known as 'Marens'. The R.M. Technical Training Depot opened at Fort Cumberland and training schools were formed at Thurlestone and Deal, with a R.M. Signals School at Saundersfoot.

The formation of the Royal Marines Commando units met with some opposition from the Army Commandos but, with the help and understanding of Admiral Lord Louis Mountbatten, the Chief of Combined Operations, the Royal Marines' special skills, which ought never to have been forgotten in such a conflict, were finally given recognition. The Commando Basic Training Centre was at Achnacarry and during 1943 six Battalions were re-organised as R.M. Commandos and trained there. A further Commando joined them in 1944 making a total of nine R.M. Commandos numbered from 40 to 48. Another important step was taken in August, 1943, when, for the first time, the Royal Marines officers of the support craft and landing craft were given power of command of these small but vital warships.

The Commando Memorial at Spean Bridge.

Badge worn on shoulder straps of tropical dress shirts 1952.

Shoulder badge worn on battle dress by all ranks not serving in Commando Units 1941-1966.

Shoulder badge worn by R.M. ranks in Army Commandos.

Shoulder badge issued unofficially to 44 (R.M.) Commando when supplies of official badge had run out.

General issue shoulder badge for all ranks in Commandos 1947-1954.

Shoulder badges issued to R.M. Commandos 1939-1945

Issue of new type shoulder badge 1946.

General issue shoulder badge for all ranks who have passed the Commando Course.

Unofficial shoulder badges worn during World War II.

Badge worn by ranks in combined operations (including Commandos) 1942-1945.

R.M. Division 1941-1943 116 Brigade (27th, 28th and 30th R.M. Battalion) 1945.

117 Brigade (31st, 32nd and 33rd Battalion) 1945.

Special Service Group 1944-1946 3rd Commando Brigade R.M. from 1946.

34th Amphibious Support Regiment 1945-1946.

104 Training Group reformed in 1943 as Royal Marines Training Brigade.

Royal Marine Engineers.

R.M. Siege Regiment 1940-1945.

The first RMFVR shoulder badge 1948.

Shoulder badge worn by ranks serving in the Royal Yacht.

Badge worn by ranks serving in Amphibious Warfare Units.

Subsequent RMFVR titles.

The Commando landings at Salerno, the first troops ashore in Italy proper. (From a painting by Charles Stadden, R.M. Museum).

Sicily and Italy

The storming of the first outlying citadel of Hitler's 'Fortress Europe' was spearheaded by the Royal Marines. Sicily was the logical stepping stone from the North African coast to Italy and the invasion of this island, code-named 'Husky', took place on July 10th, 1943. Two Royal Marines Commandos, Nos. 40 and 41, were given the task of being the first seaborne troops ashore on the southern tip of Sicily in order to silence the coastal defences overlooking the main landing beaches upon which the 1st Canadian Division was to disembark. They were to land on the narrow beach between the twin headlands of Punta Ciriga and Punta Castellazzo; this beach became known as 'Commando Cove'.

40 R.M. Commando, led by Lieutenant-Colonel J.C. Manners, R.M., was to land on this beach and clear the coast as far as Solarino. 41 R.M. Commando, led by Lieutenant-Colonel B.J.D. Lumsden, R.M., was to land, scale the cliffs and destroy strong points to the westward. Both Commandos were then to consolidate their positions and form the left flank of the main landing beachhead.

The whole operation passed off perfectly; there was hardly any resistance to the landings and by dawn both Commando forces had achieved their objectives and were pushing inland towards Spaccoforno. One commando said at the time, 'The whole process seemed fantastically deliberate and leisurely. It was hard to believe that this land beneath us, the first we had trodden since leaving Britain, was enemy soil, the first bastion of the fortress of Europe'.

Following this easy initiation, the Coastal and A.A. Artillery of M.N.D.B.O.2 moved into Augusta and Syracuse. 40 Commando next took part in the landings on the Italian mainland proper, and although by this time, September 7th, 1943, Italy had thrown in the towel, the Germans were fighting hard. 40 Commando landed at Vibo Valentino in Calabria on the northern side of the toe of Italy. This unit was also heavily engaged in the subsequent fighting on the eastern coast of Italy, when the Eighth Army crossed the Biferno river from Foggia. They landed west of Termoli and attacked the town from the rear. 'A' troop under Lieutenant D.P. Hill R.M. rushed the German H.Q. building in the town and after a very sharp spate of hand-to-hand fighting, during which twenty German paratroops were killed, the Marines took the surrender of the German colonel and thirty men.

At first light on the morning of October 2nd, the Royal Marines were posted along the road to Guglioneri. 'P' troop, under Captain Marshall, was counter-attacked by the Germans who had recovered from their surprise but broke it up with a bayonet and Bren-gun attack on their own.

Meanwhile on the other coast of Italy the Allies had invaded at Salerno and here 41 Commando under Colonel Lumsden was one of the first units

The Tom Hunter V.C., Memorial Bell at Lympstone. (C.T.C., R.M. Lympstone).

into the beachhead on the night of the 9th September, 1943. They took the town of Vietri on the way north to Naples and took up positions at the mouth of the vital pass. At dawn the Germans launched a series of determined assaults to take this position and the small force of Commandos were hard pressed. With 'A' troop almost overwhelmed in the first attack the situation was remedied by a counter-attack by 'Q' troop, led by Captain Martin Scott, R.M., during which he was killed at the head of his men. His two section commanders were also hit, Lieutenant David Lloyd, R.M. died while Lieutenant Peter Haydon, R.M. was seriously wounded and losses were heavy. Haydon, although hit in the thigh by a fragment of mortar bomb, refused to be pulled back and alone killed ten of the enemy with a rifle taken from a dead Marine. He was wounded again, but still alive when the commandos reached him once more. Nineteen years old, Haydon was the youngest officer of the Corps to receive the D.S.O. in the war.

After further fighting in the Salerno perimeter 41 Commando was withdrawn to England for refitting prior to the Normandy landings. During its weeks in Italy this unit had suffered very severe casualties. They were replaced by 43 Commando under Lieutenant-Colonel R.W.B. Simonds, R.M., who took part in the Anzio landings in January, 1944. After this they fought together with 40 R.M. Commando at the crossing of the Garigliano river.

By the early summer of 1944 both units had been transferred to the Adriatic coast once more and were based on Vis, where they carried out raids on the German-held islands off the coast of Yugoslavia in conjunction with Tito's partisans. The largest attack these units made was against Brać between June 1st and 4th, 1944. Brać is an island opposite Split on the Yugoslav coast and the intention was to divert the Germans attentions away from Tito who was under heavy attack in his mountain stronghold. The two R.M. Commando units lost heavily in this action, among the dead being Lieutenant-Colonel Manners himself. 43 R.M. Commando continued to operate in Yugoslavia until January, 1945, when, with the influence of the approaching Russian army predominant, they were pulled out.

40 R.M. Commando had meanwhile been operational in Albania and Corfu during the German withdrawal from the Balkans. Their final operations were at Lake Comacchio on the Italian mainland in April, 1945. 40 R.M. Commando led by Lieutenant-Colonel R.W. Sankey, R.M. and 43 R.M. Commando under Lieutenant-Colonel I.H. Riches, R.M., were both heavily involved. On 2nd April, when 43 Commando was held up by a nest of German machine-guns, Corporal Tom Hunter won the only V.C. awarded to the Marines in this war, when he gallantly attacked single-handed and was killed firing his Bren from the hip.

Into Europe

The invasion of Normandy, to take place on June 6th, 1944, now dominated the planning of the Royal Marines. To obtain the necessary manpower to provide crews for the innumerable landing craft and the beach obstruction clearance units, port parties, signal parties and base and administration detachments connected with Operation 'Overlord' the two M.N.B.D.O.'s were broken up. The A.A. components of these formations became the 5th R.M. A.A. Brigade under Brigadier J.E. Leech-Porter, R.M. Meanwhile the battalions of the R.M. Division had re-assumed a more traditional role as Commandos.

The re-organisation of the Division helped in this also, and the artillery component provided an Armoured Support Group equipped with *Centaur* tanks under Lieutenant-Colonel J. Harvey, R.M. Thus when the historic landing took place, the Royal Marines mounted the greatest effort in their history with some 17,500 men, almost twice their pre-war strength. In addition there were numerous R.M. gun crews in the vast fleet of warships which provided covering fire throughout the month.

In the actual landings 45 R.M. Commando under Lieutenant-Colonel N.C. Ries, R.M., landed on the left of the assault to take and secure the crossings of the Orne and reached Merville. 41 (Lieutenant-Colonel T.M. Gray, R.M.), 46 (Lieutenant-Colonel C.R. Hardy, R.M.), 47 (Lieutenant-Colonel C.F. Phillips, R.M.) and 48 (Lieutenant-Colonel J.L. Moulton, R.M.), went ashore on the main beaches, 41 and 48 took Langrune and the Douvres wireless station after heavy fighting. 48 Commando had only been formed three months before but performed valiantly. Running in under St. Aubin-sur-Mer it suffered thirty percent casualties by the time it reached the assembly area. In two days fighting, with support from the tanks of the Armoured Support Group, they took the strongest German position, the redoubt of Langrune, but emerged with less than half their strength. 41 Commando divided into two parties after landing and was heavily engaged, losing Major Barclay killed and Captains Stratford and Morris, the troop commanders, wounded. In heavy fighting they eventually took the strongpoint of Lion-sur-Mer, though not before Lieutenant-Colonel Gray and eight others had been wounded and three killed in a bombing attack.

46 Commando landed on D+1 and were told to take Petit-Enfer, another German defensive position, which they did, and then pushed on to La Délivrande, two miles inland.

47 Commando was assigned the very tough nut of Port-en-Bessin. This small French port would have been ideal for some limited unloading facilities for the invading armies on the western flank of the beach-head.

The Germans had realised this and had fully fortified the town and surrounding area. It could not be stormed frontally so 47 Commando planned to land to the east of the town and make a flank assault from Le Hamel. Heavily engaged by German shore batteries on the run-in, the fourteen landing craft were diverted some distance east of their landing area and several craft were lost. 47 Commando thus went ashore with a third of its specialist equipment gone and some casualties. The rendezvous and assembly point, the village of La Rosiere, was still held by the German defenders when they arrived, which further upset the programme. After resting the night the attack went in after a softening-up bombardment by warships and bombers at dawn on the 7th June. Heavy fighting continued all day but the town remained in German hands and they counter-attacked across 47 Commando's flanks. The turning point of their fortunes came with a surprise night attack on the main surviving German strong point by a party led by Captain T.F Cousins, during which he was killed. By morning the fortress had fallen.

H.M.S. *Quebec* at Inveraray, 1944, where landing craft crews for D-Day were trained. (From the painting by Major W.G. Goldsmith, V.R.D., R.M.R., R.M. Museum).

After the break-out from the bridge-head the Commando Brigades continued to fight along the Allies' left flank up the coast to Dunkirk. Their compatriots afloat in the small landing craft and boats were fully extended patrolling the 'Trout' line of defences to protect the vast assembly of merchant ships from German light craft and 'human torpedo' type attacks throughout July and August. However, as the land campaign moved up into the Low Countries, an even greater test awaited them in the cold dark waters of the Dutch river Scheldt that autumn.

Walcheren

Although the advance of the Allied armies towards the German frontier was beset by only a few setbacks before the onset of winter, the Germans were successful in retaining their hold on the Channel ports. Their garrisons held out most stubbornly against overwhelming odds and while they sat tight in the ports the Allied land advance slowed down, due to lack of sufficient supplies to maintain their momentum. This was particularly true in the sector where the great port of Antwerp had been captured but could not be used because the Germans held strongly fortified islands along the route of the Scheldt. The main garrisons were at South Beveland and Walcheren. While the Army attacked and reduced the former, the Royal Marines made a great contribution to the taking of the latter, a battle that was bloody and grim but which added new distinction to the Corps.

The plan of attack was for the 52nd Lowland Division to punch up from South Beveland across the causeway which connects it to the east of Walcheren island, while No. 4 Army Commando landed at Flushing in the south. The main attack to take Walcheren was to be launched from the sea against the north-western tip of the island at Westkapelle, the walls of the dyke there having been breached by bombing and most of the island having been flooded. This flooding, however, had no effect on the German gun batteries which dominated the river and so the assault had to go in where air power had failed.

To carry out the attack on Westkapelle a strong naval force of landing craft, some twenty-six equipped with guns and rockets, with a further squadron of tank landing craft, (L.C.T.'s), were to land and support the 4th Commando Brigade, which consisted of 41 R.M. Commando (Lieutenant-Colonel E.C.E. Palmer, R.M.), 47 R.M. Commando (Lieutenant-Colonel C.F. Phillips, R.M.), and 48 R.M. Commando (Lieutenant-Colonel J.L. Moulton, R.M.). The Brigade was commanded by Brigadier B.W. Leicester, D.S.O., R.M. and the close support flotilla by Captain A.F. Pugsley, D.S.O., R.N., a famous destroyer captain earlier in the war.

Further out to sea was a group of heavy warships, including the battleship *Warspite* and the monitors *Erebus* and *Roberts*, whose mighty 15-inch, one-ton, shells would add their pounding weight when called upon. The date of the attack was fixed for November 1st, 1944.

On the morning of the attack the bombers were fog-bound on their English runways so the assault went in under cover of heavy naval gunfire only. All along the dyke were German batteries, ranging in size from 8.7-inch to 3-inch guns, against which the little landing ships had no armour protection whatsoever. Notwithstanding the inequality of such a combat, Captain Pugsley took his covering Support Squadron in to point-blank range and steadily exchanged salvoes with the shore batteries. All the gun crews of these craft were Marines, and to save their comrades in the other landing craft heading for the dyke they most gallantly sacrificed themselves. By drawing most of the fire upon their own heads these men suffered very heavy losses. No less than nine craft

Royal Marines and men of the Parachute Regiment operating together in Europe during 1944. (From the painting by Leslie Cole, R.M. Museum).

were sunk and eight badly damaged and some 372 seamen and Marines were casualties.

General Eisenhower was to write of this one-sided battle:

> '......great credit for the success of the amphibious operations is largely due to the support craft of the British Navy, which unhesitatingly and in the highest traditions of the service attracted to themselves the point-blank fire of the land batteries, thus permitting the Commandos and assault troops to gain the shore with much lighter casualties than otherwise would have been the case'.

The assault plan called for 48 Commando to land on the south edge of the breach and move to Zouteland while 41 Commando went north as far as Domburg. 47 would then pass through and link up with No. 4 Army Commando driving north from Flushing. Under heavy and accurate fire, plans began to go awry. 48 Commando captured a radar station according to plan but were held by battery W.13 manned by German naval gunners and protected by minefields. Lacking fire support, an initial attack by 'Y' troop was swept away and Major D.R. de Stacpoole, R.M., was killed. Moulton called in artillery bombardment and rocket strikes by Typhoon aircraft and by nightfall the Commandos were inside the strongpoint.

41 Commando had similar problems with another battery, W.15, but attacks reduced it and by nightfall they had reached Domburg as planned, though with some losses. The next day 47 Commando passed through 48 after it had secured Zouteland village, but once again, with limited room to fight, they came up against a strongly fortified German battery, W.11. The first attack resulted in all the troop commanders becoming casualties, and the attack south came to a halt. It took a further day of very severe fighting, with artillery support from the mainland and help from 48 Commando, before this strongpoint, gallantly defended by its German garrison, was forced to surrender. At noon the German Commandant surrendered and the Commandos linked up with No. 4 Army Commando at last, on November 3rd, 1944.

With the fall of this island, minesweepers started work on clearing the Scheldt but the Germans subjected Antwerp itself to an intense bombardment by V.1 rocket-bombs in an attempt to make it untenable to the Allies. To help in the anti-aircraft defence of the city, the 5th R.M. A.A. Brigade was brought forward from Cherbourg and the A.A. defences of Antwerp came under the control of this brigade. The 1st Heavy A.A. Regiment had been employed for a time as part of the 2nd Canadian Division in the land fighting along the southern shores of the Scheldt, firing air-bursts over German positions on the far bank.

For the rest of the war in Europe, up to the German surrender in May, 1945, the Royal Marines were well in evidence. The 5th R.M. A.A. Brigade moved to Ostend and engaged German midget submarines towards the war's end, surely one of the most unusual targets ever engaged by anti-aircraft guns! The 1st Commando Brigade pushed through Holland in the bleak January of 1945 and fought a sharp, bitter action at the Montforter-beek Brook on the 23rd. They took part in the crossing of the Rhine on March 23rd at Wesel. At this time the Brigade consisted of 45 R.M. Commando (Lieutenant-Colonel W.N. Gray, R.M.), and 46 R.M. Commando (Lieutenant-Colonel T.M. Gray, R.M.), and the two commanding officers were brothers. They were at Osnabruck on April 3rd and went across the Weser four days later. After that they took part in the Aller and Elbe crossings, pressing deeper into Germany. By V.E. Day they had reached the Baltic coast at Lübeck.

A severe manpower shortage in the army meant that landing craft crews had to be retrained as infantry and sent to Germany. In this manner were formed 27, 28 and 30 Battalions R.M., who fought under Brigadier C.F. Phillips in 116 Brigade on the Maas and at Oldenburg, 33 Battalion of 117 Brigade was flown to Germany and so Royal Marines took part in the final surrender of German ports and harbour installations. But before the end of World War II could be celebrated one more enemy had to be defeated, and here also, the Royal Marines were well represented.

Victory in the East

With the departure of Force 'Viper' in 1942, as described earlier, the whole of the Far Eastern theatre was in the melting pot as the Japanese army surged forward towards the great Indian plains. It took two years of hard fighting, with scant resources and little encouragement, before General Slim's 14th Army was able to go over to the offensive once more. This was in February, 1944, and as always, the Royal Marines were in evidence.

Brigadier W.I. Nonweiler's 3rd Special Service Brigade which included 42 and 44 Commandos, R.M. were first transferred to the Burma theatre of operations in late 1943. It was blooded against the Japanese, and the jungle, in March the following year. On the 11th of that month 44 Commando carried out an attack against the coastal village of Alethangyaw. Under the command of Lieutenant-Colonel Horton, the Royal Marines Commandos landed in three waves from improvised landing craft through heavy surf just before midnight with no opposition. Strong resistance was met in the first assault on the village but the Marines cut the Japanese line of retreat next morning and inflicted some heavy losses on the enemy when they pulled back. Further confused fighting took place during the next two days before the raiders withdrew.

On January 3, 1945, 42 and 44 Commandos, under Brigadier Campbell

Hardy, D.S.O., R.M. went in with the Akyab island invasion force only to find the island had been abandoned by the Japanese. As the Japanese were withdrawing from their positions the two Commandos were re-embarked and then sent ashore at Myebon some thirty miles down the coast to cut off their retreat. Here the Royal Marines met fierce opposition with an alerted enemy waiting for them. At the village of Kangaw the Commandos landed on a mud bank, crossed mangrove swamps and engaged in bitter hand-to-hand fighting on the vital Hill 70. The hill won, it was then held by 42 Commando and 1 Army Commando against strong counter-attacks which lasted until 1st February. It was during these coastal operations that the Royal Marines Engineers attached to 3 Commando Brigade proved themselves invaluable and earned the praise of General Slim himself for their work in terrible conditions.

On January 23rd it was the turn of the Royal Marines embarked in the ships of the growing East Indies Fleet to take their place. In November, 1944, they had been landed and had undergone a month's intensive training in jungle warfare. Admiral Somerville was eager to use his Marines in an aggressive role but in December they returned to their ships. However this was only a temporary delay for the whole force, led by Colonel P. Picton-Phillipps, were landed, under the covering fire of the fleet's bombardment, on the island of Cheduba. Some 500 Royal Marines stormed ashore only to find an anti-climax, for the Japanese had fled leaving only bewildered natives. Fighting patrols were sent out to trap the enemy, one marching 34 miles in 24 hours in difficult country, but they were just too late. The whole force re-embarked on 28th, January, but were to have a crack at the Japanese when they served in some of the gun turrets during the fleet's bombardment of Ramree Island.

Meanwhile 44 Commando had moved up country and operated for a while with a complement of fifty elephants. What with the 'Horse Marines' of the 19th century, then the camels of the Sudan and now the elephants of Burma, there could be few surprises left for the Corps in the way of animal transport.

A whole series of landing operations followed the British advance and in these the Royal Marines were prominent. To carry out surveys and underwater reconnaissance of the innumerable creeks and inlets along the coast-line called for an amphibious force of frogmen to which the Marines contributed and a special Small Operations Group was set up under Lieutenant-Colonel Tollemache, to carry out amphibious and subversive warfare behind the lines of the retreating Japanese.

Some 900 Royal Marines were involved in the manning of the great flotilla of landing craft which carried the British Army back to Rangoon on May 2nd, 1945, and, on the Japanese collapse in August, a special force from the Fleet, Force 'Roma', was set up quickly under Lieutenant-Colonel

G. Barclay Grant, O.B.E., R.M., with 480 officers and men, to occupy Penang. This they did on August 28th, 1945, receiving the surrender of 3,000 Japanese troops. Captain Boothby commanded Force 'Boots' which took the island of Sabang off Sumatra while the Provost Company of the Royal Marines, under Major Little, had the honour to receive the surrender of the last major Japanese warship in Malayan waters when, at Singapore in August, they accepted the large Japanese destroyer *Kamikaze*, whose commander presented the ship's bugle to the Company as a mark of respect for his victors.

In the Pacific, the largest contribution Britain was able to make to the final defeat of Japan was the despatch and operation of the largest fleet of Royal Navy ships to operate in World War II, the British Pacific Fleet, Task Force 57. This fleet fought in the Okinawa campaign and Marines saw action manning anti-aircraft weapons against Japanese aircraft, while many more Royal Marines were piloting Hellcats, Corsairs and Avengers of the Fleet Air Arm in strikes against Japanese airfields and later at the

The Diploma presented to Royal Marines present at the Japanese surrender in Tokyo Bay, 1945. (R.M. Museum).

139

mainland itself. Other Marines had the chance to avenge their comrades in the *Prince of Wales* and *Repulse* when the battleship *King George V* and British cruisers took part in prolonged bombardments of the Japanese factories around Tokyo in July, 1945.

In August the British Fleet joined the Americans in Tokyo Bay for the Japanese Official Surrender which was signed aboard the U.S.S. *Missouri*. The senior officer of the Royal Marines present went ashore and hoisted the Union Jack in Yokohama. This was Major Peter Norcock, R.M., whose grandfather had served in the Royal Marines battalion which was stationed there in 1864, and later fought at Simonoseki.

A Reduced Role 1946/50

The end of the Second World War found the Corps at the highest strength it had ever achieved, some 80,000 men in all. Of this grand total some ten percent, just over 8,000 men, had been war casualties. As was the usual custom in their long history, the coming of peace saw a drastic reduction in their strength and this was coupled with considerable uncertainty about the future. With the advent of the Atomic Bomb, all the long and hard lessons of conventional warfare seemed to be in the melting pot. Certainly over the next fifteen years the strength of the Royal Navy dwindled rapidly and it continues to do so. By the mid-1950's all the battleships had gone, along with the heavy cruisers, and so the traditional role of the Royal Marines afloat vanished. It is true that in the small-ship navy of today each of the little frigates carries a Royal Marines detachment but the days of the big guns have gone for ever.

The Corps concentrated upon its Commando role, a role that was confirmed as their own province by a Parliamentary decision of October, 1945, which stated that the Army Commandos were to be disbanded and the Commando role would pass exclusively to the Royal Marines. The total Commando strength was reduced to one Brigade, and No. 3, then in Hong Kong, assumed this task. Three Commandos emerged from this cut back, Numbers 40 (formerly 44), 42 and 45, thus maintaining post-war a Commando title from each of the three theatres of war.

The old 'Divisions' vanished in the limbo of post-war retrenchment, to be replaced by geographical groups at Chatham, Portsmouth and Plymouth. In 1946 the post of Adjutant General, R.M. became instead that of Commandant General, R.M., with direct access to the Board of Admiralty, a step forward for the Corps. Centralized drafting, records, pay and N.C.O.'s promotion were introduced under General Sir Dallas Brooks.

140

By 1949 the strength of the Corps as a whole had been reduced to just over 10,000 men, which led to the abolition of the Chatham Group, whose old Divisional Colours were laid up in Rochester Cathedral. Only the centralised Pay and Records Office remained at Chatham and even this went in 1960, when it moved to Portsmouth. Thus the Corps' links with Chatham, dating back to 1664 were finally cut.

The Royal Marines Association was formed in 1946 and this organisation has thrived. To remedy the long-felt lack of trained reserves, the Royal Marine Forces Volunteer Reserve was set up in 1948, and has since become the Royal Marines Reserve. Each training centre was organised in three wings, Commando, Sea Service and Amphibious, its first establishment being for a strength of 1,500 men.

Despite the drastic reduction in its numbers, the morale of the Corps has remained high and its confidence remains unshaken. Witness the famous story of the Royal Marine in Hong Kong who was approached by a

Royal Marines uniforms for the post-war period (From the painting by Charles Stadden, R.M. Museum).

1971	1970	1970	1970	1971	1971	1972
Corporal	Cook	Senior N.C.O.	Marine	Marine Commando	Physical Training Instructor	Sniper
(Barrack Working Dress)	(Working Dress)	(Mess Dress)	(Action Working Dress)	(Arctic Kit)	(First Class)	(Operational)

1971	1969	1971	1970	1971	1971	1972
Sergeant	Musician	Despatch Rider	Frogman	Helicopter Pilot	Physical Training Instructor	Drum Major
(Raincoat)	(Black Cape)	(Working Dress)	(Operational)	(Flying Kit)	(Staff P.T.I.)	(Full Dress)

burly U.S. Marine who sneeringly enquired what the initials 'R.M.' stood for on his uniform. '*Real* Marines', was the answer he received.

The 3rd Commando Brigade Royal Marines was the trouble-shooter of the first post-war years. Between 1946 and 1947 the Brigade formed the garrison at Hong Kong but in 1947 it went to the Mediterranean to form a mobile Middle East reserve based on Malta. The movements of 3 Commando Brigade were continuous throughout this period. In January, 1948, 40 Commando was at Haifa guarding dock installations, while 42 and 45 Commandos were stationed at Tripoli to protect the Four Nations Committee on Italian Colonies. Both these units joined 40 Commando in Palestine in April, 1948, to cover the final withdrawal of British forces which took place the following month. After this, 40 Commando went to Cyprus to deal with illegal Jewish immigrants while 42 and 45 alternated between Malta and the Canal Zone. All these moves took place at short notice. Finally, in 1949, with the Communists overrunning China, all three Commandos and the H.Q. of the Brigade returned once more to Hong Kong.

The Marine who volunteered for sea! With less and less chance of serving afloat during the rapid post-war run-down of the fleet such volunteers were not so rare as this earlier Bateman cartoon makes out. (From the cartoon by Bateman, R.M. Museum).

Defeating the Terrorists

In 1950 the long drawn-out campaign of terror and intimidation that had been waged against the village communities in Malaya since the end of the Japanese occupation came to a head. The original terrorist groups, the Min Yuen and the Lie Ton Ten, had become organised more purposefully under the Communist banner as the 'Malayan National Liberation Army'. The usual pattern of wholesale murder and blackmail followed, particularly against the British planters and others who had introduced the only real wealth that the country had ever known. The killings reached such a scale that the civilian authorities were unable to cope and the troops had to go in to mount a full-scale operation. This was done with patience and limited resources, but, under the humane guidance of General Sir Gerald Templer and others, the Communists were defeated, both in the field and in the hearts of the Malayan people.

It was while the troubles were at their height that the Commandos moved into Malaya. In May and June, 1950, the H.Q., 3 Commando

Dhala Patrol. The war in southern Arabia. (From the print by David Shepperd, R.M. Museum).

Brigade and the three Commandos were transferred from Hong Kong to Malaya. 40 Commando was stationed at Kuala Kangsar in North Perak and 45 Commando at Tapah in South Perak, while 42 Commando was at Ipoh. Here they remained for two years patrolling an area of jungle, mountains and rivers, 'the size of Wales', with great success. During their period of counter-insurgency operations, which ended in April, 1952, the Brigade accounted for 171 terrorists killed and 49 captured for the loss of four Royal Marines officers and fifteen other ranks killed. The Royal Marines were awarded some eighteen decorations for this work and twenty-five Mentions in Despatches. General Sir John Harding later commented: — 'It is a record of hard work, devotion to duty and good comradeship of which the Royal Marines have every reason to be proud'. The full story of this twilight war is told in *Green Beret and Red Star*, written by Anthony Crockett, a Major in 42 Commando at the time.

Mementos of the jungle fighting. 45 Commando's 'A' sub-section, 'B' troop, after operations in Sungei Siput South, September, 1950, during the Malayan Campaign. Captured terrorist newspapers filled with hysterical propaganda contrast strangely with 45 Commando's own paper, *The Tiger Times.* (Courtesy F.J. Westwood).

On the termination of their period of duty in Malaya the Brigade returned to Malta and here, on November 29th, 1952, the three Commandos were each presented with their first colours by H.R.H. Prince Philip, Duke of Edinburgh. It was very appropriate that Prince Philip should have carried out this ceremony for the following year he became Captain-General of the Corps in succession to His Majesty King George VI.

In 1953 the Mediterranean began to seethe once more with the overthrow of the Egyptian monarchy. The British Canal Zone protecting the Suez Canal was threatened with terrorist activity and the Commando Brigade moved into the area to maintain law and order until, in August, 1954, the Brigade withdrew.

The same year further economies forced the return of one of the Commandos, No. 42, to England, where they had the opportunity to carry out an operation which made the last-ever addition to the rapidly shrinking British Empire. This was the annexing of the island of Rockall, an uninhabited rock some three hundred miles to the west of the Outer Hebrides. Two members of 42 Commando were lowered from a helicopter operating from the survey ship *Vidal* in September, 1955, to affix a plaque and a flag denoting British sovereignty.

Having withdrawn from Egypt, the British began to build up the island of Cyprus as an alternative base in the Mediterranean. This in turn led to an outbreak of the kind of terrorism which had successfully evicted us from Palestine and the Canal Zone and which, it was thought, would probably have the same effect there. The mixed population of the island, which had been under British protection since 1878, part Turk and part Greek, had often led to disturbances before but they had always been put down firmly and the two peoples co-existed quite well. However, taking advantage of the strong feeling of the Greek population for union with Greece, the EOKA campaign, the usual pattern of murder began and the military were once more called in to hunt down the killers and protect the ordinary citizens of the island. In September, 1955, H.Q., 3 Commando Brigade and 40 and 45 Commandos moved into the island to help in this task, being based at Limassol, Paphos and Troodos respectively. Here they remained until August, 1956, in an anti-terrorist role with all that it implied and again they added to the Corps' fine record of restraint and sense of duty in their thankless task.

Other policing duties came the way of the Royal Marines as the years went by. In December, 1962, a revolt broke out in Brunei, the British-protected state in the north-west of Borneo. Troops were thin on the ground and so 42 Commando was flown in at once from Singapore to assemble at Brunei Town with the 1st/2nd Gurkha Rifles, other reinforcements coming in later by sea. Their most urgent task was to effect the rescue of the Resident and other European hostages, two of them women, who were being held by the rebels at the town of Limbang. Two ancient Z-Lighters, dating back to the First World War, were found in the harbour and, manned by seamen from the minesweepers *Chawton* and *Fiskerton*, they were taken up river with 'L' Company, 42 Commando, embarked. At dawn next day, the 11th December, the two lighters approached the river front of Limbang under heavy fire and 'L' Company stormed ashore with the loss of five killed and five wounded to drive off the rebels and rescue the hostages just before they were due to be executed. The rebels were later hunted down with helicopters and river boats.

When the *Albion* arrived with H.Q., 3 Commando Brigade at Labuan, she landed 40 Commando at Kuching in Sarawak, whence they were airlifted to join 42 Commando in the jungle hunt. 145 (Maiwand) Battery of 29 Commando Regiment, Royal Artillery, later arrived with heavier support and within a week the revolt had been successfully put down. 42 Commando earned a Bar to a Military Cross, two Military Medals and three Mentions in Despatches in the course of this episode.

Aden was the next large base to be built up by Britain. The lesson that carriers, support ships and amphibious potential is the most effective and, in the long run, the cheapest method of fighting brush-fire wars was never fully accepted by any of the post-war governments and so Aden was a repeat of Palestine, Egypt and Cyprus. Communist-armed and backed terrorists began infiltrating into Aden from the Yemen during the early 1960's and 45 Commando was operational against them in the mountainous Radfan region with notable success. In April, 1964, they made a dangerous crossing and took the strong points guarding Wadi Taim. Three years of further operations ended in the evacuation of the area by the British in 1967, 42 Commando being the last troops away.

Today the terrible carnage of the terrorist bomb has come closer to home, as its success elsewhere ensured it was bound to, and it is in the streets of Belfast, Londonderry and other towns of the United Kingdom that today's young Royal Marines face the same dangers as their predecessors with equal gallantry. During the Turkish intervention in Cyprus in 1974, 40 and 41 Commandos protected British interests and civilians on the island.

The Korean War

The peninsula of Korea, for long ruled by Japan, had become artificially split into two sections after World War II when Soviet Russia, having refrained from entering the war against Japan until the final days, overran the northern part in 1945. Below the 38th Parallel Korea remained independent but above it the Communists installed a puppet regime and,

The plaque of 41 Commando and the plaque of H.Q.3 Commando Brigade. (R.M. Museum).

in defiance of a United Nations Commission set up to supervise free and fair elections (or perhaps because of it), the North Koreans invaded with their full strength, backed up by Chinese arms and equipment, on June 25th, 1950. Russia being absent from the Council Chamber, the U.N. was able to pass a resolution calling for resistance to this aggression without it being vetoed and an international force was assembled. By the time the first onslaught of the North Koreans had been checked and then reversed the Royal Marines had joined in the fighting.

Marines from the Royal Navy Task Force, assembled off the west coast, had been the first to see service in bombardments and similar occurrences, as well as limited raids, but the first large force to arrive was 41 Independent Commando, R.M., which had been specially formed at Plymouth in August, 1950, and flown to Japan in plain clothes to be equipped there by the Americans. They took part in a number of coastal raids in conjunction with the U.S. Army Special Raiding Forces.

When the U.N. forces, under General Douglas MacArthur, finally drove up the peninsula from the beach-head of Inchon and the perimeter of Pusan right up to the frontier of Red China the Chinese took a hand and poured three-quarters of a million men into Korea to decide the issue. Caught in this flood of men and machines, the U.N. force fell back. 41 Commando, under Lieutenant-Colonel D.B. Drysdale, R.M., had already undertaken some very hard fighting in the advance from Hamhung to Hagaro in November when Communist ambushes had split their column in half and caused heavy casualties. Now they were trapped with the 1st U.S.M.C. Division in the region of the Chosin Reservoirs. In the very severe fighting which followed these Marines fought their way through eight Chinese Divisions to reach the coast and safety. For this action 41 Commando was awarded the Presidential Citation, with a Battle Streamer to be borne on their Regimental Colour. The following year the unit was operational 150 miles behind the enemy lines blowing up rail links and again, in April, on the island of Wonsan before disbanding in February, 1952.

Royal Marines Museum

The Suez Operation

The new head of the Republic of Egypt, Colonel Nasser, intensified the state of armed hostility that had existed with Israel since the war of 1948 and, after forcing the expulsion of the British from the Canal Zone and nationalising the Canal, ordered that all Israeli vessels were to be banned from using it. This was in flat contradiction of the Convention of 1888 which allowed free passage to ships of all nations and Israel and Egypt soon found themselves at war. To protect the Canal itself from this twin threat and to ensure its neutrality in the future, Great Britain and France requested both combatants to withdraw from the Canal Zone but this Egypt refused to do. Armed intervention was therefore resorted to by the two western nations, but so low had their defences fallen that it required several weeks before enough aircraft, troops and shipping could be assembled to transport a modest force against Egypt. Things had certainly changed since Tel-el-Kebir and it needed an all-out effort by both

45 Commando making the first helicopter assault at Suez in 1956.
(From the painting by Lane, 45 Commando R.M.)

powers, with aircraft carriers and bombers from Cyprus, to eliminate the Egyptian air force before the invasion commenced.

Both Mediterranean Commandos returned to Malta from Cyprus and 42 Commando was hastily flown out again from England. Thus 3 Commando Brigade was once more united under the command of Brigadier R.W. Madoc, O.B.E., with 40 Commando under Lieutenant-Colonel D.G. Tweed, M.B.E., R.M., 42 Commando under Lieutenant-Colonel P.L. Norcock, O.B.E., R.M., and 45 Commando under Lieutenant-Colonel N.H. Tailyour, D.S.O., R.M. After long days of slow sailing the Allied attack finally went in on the 5th November, 1956, with a drop of paratroops on Port Fuad and Port Said.

The Egyptian forces consisted of some 75,000 troops, 300 tanks and 300 Russian-built aircraft, but the majority of the latter had been put out of action and the land forces had proved completely ineffective against the Israelis. Therefore, when the Allied assault finally made its ponderous way to the beaches, it was against indifferent resistance and the initial objectives were soon taken.

The seaborne attack began at dawn on November 6th against Port Said. 42 Commando, landing with amphibious vehicles and tank support, soon linked up with the French while 40 Commando also assaulted by sea and began to clear the town of its defenders in a street by street operation in which it suffered some casualties. More spectacular was the helicopter assault made by 45 Commando from the British Carrier Task Force some seven miles out to sea. Operating from the light fleet carriers *Ocean* and *Theseus* the Commando was ferried ashore in the helicopters of 845 Fleet Air Arm Squadron. Although helicopters had been used earlier in a small way in Malaya, this Suez landing was the first opposed helicopter assault and so, once more, the Royal Marines made history.

In all, some twenty-two helicopters landed 400 men and 23 tons of stores in ninety minutes near to the Casino Pier, thus effectively demonstrating the capability of this method of quick troop lifting under fire. The combined Allied force now ashore, reinforced by the 6th Royal Tank Regiment, then pushed rapidly on down the Canal and had penetrated some twenty-three miles against feeble opposition when the word came for a halt while the Allies complied with a hastily prepared United Nations resolution to stop fighting. By December all the Allied forces had been withdrawn.

This campaign was something of a water-shed in British defence policy for after it all forms of conventional amphibious assault were looked upon as being slow and obsolete. Fortunately the speed of the helicopter assault presented a contrast and this method was adopted for future forms of Commando work with the fleet.

Confrontation

Perhaps the most serious, certainly the most protracted, of the 'brush-fire' wars with which the Royal Marines have been associated since Korea was the period of confrontation with Indonesia, a state of war without declaration by either side. This rambling republic, which consisted of the thousands of islands and groups of islands of the former Dutch East Indies, was ruled over by a highly nationalistic President who, backed by Communist influences and arms, began to cast his eyes on the British protectorates of Sarawak, Brunei and Sabah in Borneo.

Open warfare was out of the question but the usual well-tried pattern of infiltration and terrorism was put into motion once again and the same response saw British forces carrying out jungle patrols from fortresses carved out of the forests. It was a snipers war, a campaign of sudden ambush, brief and bitter skirmishes and, finally, of unpublicised attrition with the British forces again operating on a shoe-string.

The Limbang landing, Brunei, 1962. (From the print by Terence Cuneo, R.M. Museum).

The Royal Marines were responsible for policing over 30,000 square miles of territory with units spread 170 miles apart. Much of this area was virgin jungle interlaced with river and swamp. The main river of Sarawak could accommodate an Inshore Minesweeper for over one hundred miles from the sea thus enabling amphibious operations to be mounted deep in the hinterland. The ill-defined border could not be crossed by British troops thus giving the aggressors all the advantages of choosing their own terrain.

On Malayasia Day, August 31st, 1965, a large patrol from 'B' Company, 40 Commando, collided with an Indonesian platoon which had crossed to their side of the border. In the resulting fire-fight six Indonesians were killed and four wounded. One Marine was wounded. The ability to bring down devastating fire quickly is the key to success in such jungle battles and the emphasis was placed on individual marksmanship.

Between 1963 and 1966, when the Indonesian Government finally called off the campaign and a new era of friendly relations began between the two countries, 40 and 42 Commandos operated several tours of duty, based at Tawau and Kuching. In support they had the guns of the Commando Light Regiment and, for air-lift operations, the helicopters of 845 and 848 R.N. Air Squadrons were on hand.

The Royal Marines in the sky

The passing of the big-gun ships has already been noted, as has the decline in the effectiveness of the slow forms of amphibious assault. The future of the Corps, therefore, without doubt lay increasingly in the air, even though the end of the aircraft carrier, as the main unit of the fleet, was being announced. Due to the proven versatility of the helicopter, coupled with the progressive reduction of what few overseas bases remained to us, it was decided to adopt a limited form of 'mobile task force' in order to deal with small outbreaks and disturbances, known as the 'brush-fire' type of incident. These forces, comprising a small carrier equipped with a commando unit and helicopters, escorted by frigates with modern assault ships and logistic ships, could not hope to overawe any major power but this was not seen as their function.

Already the Royal Marines were beginning to adapt to their new aerial role and in 1961, for example, Lieutenant Roger Learoyd, R.M., became the first R.M. officer to join an operational squadron as a fully qualified helicopter pilot. The helicopter carrier had come into being in 1957 when the light carrier *Bulwark* was first taken in hand for conversion into a helicopter carrier (now known as LPH to conform with American designations). By 1960 the ship, stripped of her aircraft and guns and with her hangars fitted out to accommodate 600 Royal Marines Commandos, a squadron of helicopters, vehicles, assault craft and stores, was ready and 42 Commando, with their colours, embarked for their first Far Eastern tour of duty. The *Bulwark* was based on Singapore and H.Q. 3rd Commando Brigade duly moved there from Malta in April, 1961.

40 Commando remained at Malta and 45 Commando was serving in Aden so, in order to provide a reserve force Commando unit for afloat support, 41 Commando was re-formed at Bickleigh in March, 1960, and the following year saw the re-establishment of 43 Commando as well and the strength of each was increased to 687 officers and men. Artillery support was initially provided by the 105mm pack howitzers of the 29th Regiment, Royal Artillery, so that, after a gap of over one hundred and fifty years, the Royal Artillery again went to sea in H.M. Ships. The wheel had come full circle.

The first test of this new type of formation took place in June, 1961, when Iraq threatened to annex the neighbouring oil-rich nation of Kuwait.

A Royal Marines helicopter assault group on the deck of a Commando Carrier. (Royal Marines Official).

The ruler of Kuwait called for British help against this aggression and fortunately the *Bulwark* was in the Persian Gulf at the time. Within twenty-four hours 42 Commando was being flown in to man defences along the Kuwait/Iraq border. The Amphibious Warfare Squadron was also on hand and armoured support began to be unloaded. On July 2nd the small R.M. detachment from one of the frigates on station, the *Loch Alvie*, joined 42 Commando and by the next day 45 Commando were airlifted in from Aden. This proved to be enough, and, although further units joined them, Iraqi plans had been thwarted within a week.

In April, 1962, a second commando carrier, the *Albion*, was commissioned and sailed for the Far East to relieve the *Bulwark*. 40 Commando subsequently took part briefly in the Brunei revolt and the confrontation with Indonesia as already described. Meanwhile yet another chance was given for the Royal Marines to show their worth when, in January, 1964, widespread mutinies by East African armies led President Nyerere of Tanganyika to call for British help. Although both commando carriers were far away, fortunately a sister ship, still acting in her proper role as an operational carrier, the *Centaur*, was able to embark 45 Commando and, at first light on the morning of the 25th January, flew them in to Dar-es-Salaam where they quickly put down a mutinous battalion at the Colito barracks. Others were flown inland to Tabora and Natchingwea while *Centaur's* jets patrolled overhead. Within a few days it was all over and peace was restored, and 45 were subsequently relieved by 41 Commando airlifted from the U.K.

Since that time the Commando ship has continued to feature in the fleet although *Bulwark*, *Albion* and *Hermes* are now very old ladies indeed with no sign of modern replacements. In 1964 the Tercentenary of the formation of the Lord Admiral's Regiment was celebrated and Her Majesty the Queen dined with Royal Marines officers at Greenwich and reviewed the Royal Marines in the grounds of Buckingham Palace. 310 years of history finds the Royal Marines today still very much an active front-line force. Since the end of the Second World War, the Marines have made more than sixty landings in the cause of peace and over 120 Royal Marines have been killed on active service.

At work and play

What of the Royal Marines of today? They are probably the most highly trained and versatile of all our armed forces and, although their numbers are desperately small, their strength is out of all proportion to their size. Today the Marine is a thinking, as well as a fighting, man and this is important. The Corps is renowned for its special brotherhood and also for its discipline, but discipline today is attuned to intelligence and coupled with the finest military training yet devised. The result is a tough, hard, but aware, fighting man and the unique versatility of the Corps is, in itself, an attraction to the right type of man.

The Corps has three main functions; it provides the Commando forces which are ready to go into action anywhere in the world in the best traditions of the service, and today's Commandos go in fast; it provides this nation's most experienced and battle-ready amphibious forces, together with their associated equipment and back-up facilities; and it provides, in the old manner, the traditional, limited, sea-going detachments for service with the fleet.

Under these three main headings the scope and diversity for any Royal Marine is enormous, as the accompanying illustrations clearly show. A Royal Marine can find himself piloting a helicopter, steering a landing craft towards a hostile beach, in charge of a beach-control party unloading vital equipment (as in the case of the East Pakistan floods a few years

Commandos storm ashore from their Gemini assault craft. (Royal Marines Official).

154

ago), or parachuting into the water as a member of the Special Boat Section.

As a frogman, he could be reconnoitring uncharted coastlines and positions. He could be scaling mountain peaks or cliffs in Scotland or Austria, roping down into the Malaysian jungle ready for patrol, or swimming underwater in the Indian Ocean. The Royal Marines have canoe teams in the tradition of the 'Cockleshell Heroes', ski patrols out in the wastes of Norway guarding NATO's northern flank, and they train all the snipers for the armed forces, being skilled in the arts of stealth and marksmanship. As a musician, he could find himself playing at the Royal Tournament in London or in a Tokyo park to an equally admiring audience.

The key to their self-reliance and efficiency is of course fitness and in the field of sporting activity the Royal Marines are unsurpassed.

The Corps have made a great contribution as an integral part of the Royal Navy teams in all sporting events and this is typified by the fact

Arctic Commandos lying in ambush on exercise in Norway, 1973. (Royal Marines Official).

Royal Marines canoes landing assault frogmen during exercises. (Royal Marines Official).

Number One Raiding Squadron, Royal Marines, in action. (Royal Marines Official).

Royal Marines landing craft entering the dock of an Assault Ship. (Royal Marines Official).

A beach survey by Royal Marines frogmen. (Royal Marines Official).

A Royal Marines shipborne detachment disembarking from a frigate. (Royal Marines Official).

A patrol covers a tropical beach during excercises in the West Indies. (Royal Marines Official).

that Lieutenant Andy Higginson, R.M., captained the Royal Navy team which in 1974 defeated both the Army and the Royal Air Force teams in the Inter-Services Rugby Football tournament. And so it is as part of the Naval teams that Royal Marines usually feature, although the Royal Marines produced their own Field Gun teams at the Royal Tournament in London between 1919 and 1934.

The Royal Marines by virtue of their training and duties become experts in a number of sporting events. Warrant Officer T. Shenton for example is the British National Coach in canoeing and Corporal T. Alan-Williams achieved international class in this sport. Orienteering is another recent sport which is particularly adapted to the Corps. Cross-country running over unknown territory with map and compass through a series of check points is a gruelling test of stamina and each year the Royal Marines hold a special contest against the United States Marine Corps in friendly competition. Both Lieutenant J.J. Thompson and Lieutenant M.H. Wells-Cole have been outstanding in this event. In athletics

Norway, February, 1973. 45 Commando. (45 Commando, R.M.).

Jungle warfare training. Landing by helicopter in a small clearing. (Royal Marines Official).

A ski-patrol leader confers with his helicopter pilot during Arctic excercises in 1973. (Royal Marines Official).

Sergeant J. Douglas set the British Record for 1500 metres in 1972 and fellow Sergeants J. Watts and E.J. Kelland are also eminent. With Commando training, it is not unexpected that Captain G. Sherridan is a highly-rated skiing expert. The long-range version of this sport, Biathlon, was represented in the Corps by Major R. Tuck and Colour-Sergeant M. Halliday and in sport parachuting Sergeant A. Skennerton and Marine R.E. Higgins skills are of top quality and expertise.

Other representatives who have achieved International standards in their sports in recent years include Sergeant F. Cummings (Judo), Band Sergeant D.J. Moore (Sailing), Captain S.H.B. Cook and Second Lieutenant R.D.S. Martin (Hockey), Major H.N. Cooper (Shooting), Lieutenant R.A.S. Spiers (Bobsleigh), and it is not suprising either to learn that in 1966 Marine D. Finnegan was the England breast-stroke champion in swimming. The Devizes to Westminster annual canoe race has been won by the Corps 15 years out of 25. These are achievements of which the Royal Marines are justly proud.

Landing craft putting ashore heavy equipment. (Royal Marines Official).

A Royal Marine's Miscellany

The present badge of the Royal Marines, the Globe and Laurel surmounted by the Lion and the Crown, is by no means the only badge worn by the Corps during its long history. The Foul Anchor, the badge of the Lord High Admiral, was worn for the first time in 1747. The Laurel is said to have been awarded for the distinguished work of the Marines during the capture of Belle Isle in 1761.

The motto *Per Mare Per Terram* (By Sea By Land) is believed to have first been used at the Battle of Bunker Hill during the War of American Independence in 1775. It was on this occasion that General Howe advanced his troops against the American fortifications twice in the face of heavy fire and was repulsed. The 47th of the Line, with the two battalions of Marines led by Major Pitcairn, then advanced and met similar heavy fire during which Pitcairn was killed. The line wavered and almost broke but with the cry, 'Break then, and let the Marines pass

Royal Marines Officers mounting vigil in Westminster Abbey during Sir Winston Churchill's lying in State. (From the painting by Mrs. Mary Young, R.M. Museum).

through you', the British stormed forward, taking the hill, but with the loss of over a thousand dead.

The Corps nickname of 'The Jollies' originated with the Trained Bands of London, who had this nickname in 1660. Whereas the citizen soldiers took the name 'Tame Jollies' the Marines were called 'Royal Jollies'. 'Leathernecks' is another name originally associated with the Corps, being derived from the leather stock they once wore. This name has been adopted by the United States Marines, whilst the Royal Marines are better known as 'Bootnecks', from the old sailors saying 'Take your seaboots off my neck'.

Another traditional name applied was 'Joe' or 'Joey' from the jingle 'I'm Joe the Marine, I'm *always* gay and hearty, *When* I'm not for Guard, I'm in the working party'. The old nickname *Lobsters* was obviously derived from their scarlet tunics. The equally outdated word *Pongoes* once applied to the Marines, although in this century it is applied by the Royal Navy to all soldiers. The original battalion to earn this name in the early

Ex-Royal Marines serving as Yeomen of the Guard are pictured here with General Sir Ian Gourlay, K.C.B., O.B.E., M.C., and Major-General R.B. Loudoun, C.B., O.B.E., at St. James's Palace. (Royal Marines Official).

1800's was based at Chatham, where the units serving overseas drafted their superfluous men. Another nickname quoted by Colonel G.W.M. Grover, O.B.E., in his excellent *Short History of the Royal Marines*, is *Cheeks the Marine*. This, states Colonel Grover, was the Marine equivalent of the Army's *Thomas Atkins*, a fictitious Marine, born on the muster roll, whose pay went to Greenwich Naval Hospital.

The Corps has a number of Memorable Dates when a fanfare is sounded at noon. These fanfares were once sounded on silver memorial bugles carried in memory of R.M.L.I. officers killed during the Great War. Until 1950, the Corps celebrated sixteen of these days but these were then reduced to six, which are:

April 23rd.	The Raid on Zeebrugge, 1918, during the Great War.
June 7th.	The Battle for Belle Isle, 1761, during the Seven Years War.
July 24th.	The Capture of Gibraltar, 1704, during the War of the Spanish Succession.
October 21st.	The Battle of Trafalgar, 1805, during the Napoleonic Wars.
October 28th.	The Corps Birthday, 1664.
November 1st.	The Assault on Walcheren, 1944, during the Second World War.

Operational units also observe their own special days which are:

January 23rd.	Attack of Montforterbeek, 1945.	45 Commando.
January 31st.	Battle of Kangaw, 1945.	42 Commando.
June 6th.	Normandy Landings, 1944.	Landing Craft Squadrons.
August 19th.	Raid on Dieppe, 1942.	40 Commando.
September 9th.	The Salerno Landings, 1943.	41 Commando.

The Presentation of the Colours and the Badge

By 1827 it had become the practice in Army Infantry Regiments to have their battle honours emblazoned on their regimental colours. It was therefore natural that the Royal Marines should follow the same custom and so, when new colours were due for presentation to the four Divisions, a list of honours, to which the Corps was entitled, was submitted to King George IV. The number of honours considered worthy of being carried on the colours were so numerous that the king made a unique compromise.

And so it was that on 26th September, 1827, H.R.H. The Duke of Clarence, who was presenting the colours to Chatham Division on behalf of his monarch addressed the parade as follows: —

'His Majesty has selected for you the badge which I this day, by his permission, present to you, a badge which you have hardly and honourably earned. From the difficulty of selecting any number of places to inscribe on these standards, your sovereign has been pleased to give them "The Great Globe itself", as their properest and most distinctive badge. He also directed that his own name (George IV) shall be added to that peculiar badge, The Anchor, which is your distinctive bearing, in order that it may be known hereafter that George the Fourth had conferred on you the honourable and well earned badge this day presented to you'.

A Royal Marines officer's helmet plate. (R.M. Museum).

Officers with the Colours of the Royal Marines, 1833.
(From the print in *Costumes of the Royal Navy and Royal Marines*, 1833).

Thus it was that the 'Globe encircled with Laurel' was the very appropriate choice of the monarch for the Corps whose duty has taken them to every part of the world. His Majesty also directed that whatever monarch the Corps might subsequently serve, the Cypher·G IV R was to 'forever appear'.

The existing motto of the time, *Per Mare Per Terram*, was also given firm approval and was allowed to remain. 'Surmounting the entire is the word GIBRALTAR, in commemoration of the important national services you performed there.' Thus the Colours have remained to this day, with the Cypher of the reigning monarch in the centre of the Queen's Colours. However, the Regimental Colours still bear King George IV's Cypher in the centre.

The Colours, a general history

The illustrations in this section clearly show the changes that the colours have undergone over three centuries. In 1664 every regiment had several colours, one for each company, the senior of which carried the Colonel's colour, the next the Lieutenant-Colonel's and so on. The original colours of the Admiral's Regiment reflected the yellow and crimson of their uniforms and it is of particular interest to note that 42 Commando R.M. today still use the design of the original Lieutenant Colonel's colour as their unit flag.

By the time the six Marine regiments were formed in 1739 the number of colours carried by each regiment had been reduced to two, a King's

Colour, which was the Union Flag and a Second or Regimental Colour to match the facings of the Regiment. By 1760 the basic field of the regimental colour of each of the Marine Divisions was white, with the addition of the foul anchor symbol, first worn some years earlier; this was surmounted by a wreath of roses and thistles and the Union Flag in the upper canton. With the granting of the title Royal in 1802 the field of the Regimental Colour conformed with the facings of a Royal Regiment and became the dark blue with St. Patrick's cross added to the Union Flag.

With the granting of the Globe and the Cypher of King George IV the design of the colours of the Royal Marines remained standardised up to the present day, except for those presented to each Division in 1858 with very little ceremony. These were not popular and were replaced.

Today, Queen's and Regimental colours are carried by each of the four Commandos. The first stands of Colours were initially presented on 29th November, 1952, to 40, 42 and 45 Commandos, R.M. by H.R.H. Prince Philip, Duke of Edinburgh, in Malta and a stand was presented to 41 Commando soon after their being reformed. The Queen's Colour is the Union Flag, with the foul anchor in the centre and the Cypher of H.M. the Queen interlaced. Above is the St. Edward's Crown surmounted by the

1. The Colonel's Colour.

2. The Lieutenant-Colonel's Colour.

3. The Major's and the Companies' Colours.

4. Colour of Capt. Charles Middleton's Company in the Virginia Expedition of 1676.

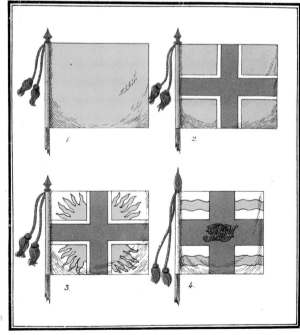

The Colours 1664-1689. (From the print in Edye's *History of the Royal Marine Forces*).

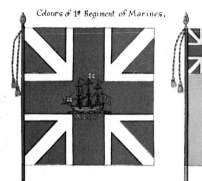
Colours of 1st Regiment of Marines, 1739 — 1748.

The Colours 1739-1748. 1760. (From *Random Records of the Royal Marines*).

1760

1810.

1827.

The Colours 1810. 1827. (From *Random Records of the Royal Marines*).

168

scroll inscribed 'Gibraltar', while underneath is the 'Great Globe' surrounded by a laurel wreath and below this is the scroll inscribed 'Per Mare Per Terram'.

The Regimental Colour is a blue flag with a small Union flag in the canton nearest the top of the colour pike. In the centre is the foul anchor and Cypher of King George IV whilst the Cypher of H.M. the Queen surmounted by a crown appears in the other three corners. Each unit has its own numerical designations below the motto on their Regimental Colours. The gold tassels on the colour pikes have interwoven thread of the unit colour worn as lanyards; 40 - light blue; 41 - yellow; 42 - white; and 45 Commando R.M. - red.

The Corps Colours when worn horizontally show the following significance and proportion: *Yellow* (1 part) 1664 colour. *Green* (1 part) Light Infantry colour. *Red* (2 parts) Tunic colour until 1876. *Blue* (8 parts) Association with Royal Navy.

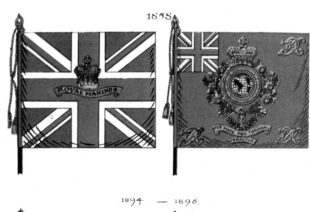

The Colours 1858. 1894-96. (From *Random Records of the Royal Marines*).

169

Bands and Marches

It was in 1847 that the rating of Bandsman was introduced into the Royal Navy although of course R.M. Divisional bands had existed long before that. In 1903 the Corps became responsible for bands in the Royal Navy and the Royal Naval School of Music was established at Eastney. The incorporation of a lyre on their badges identified them, until their amalgamation in 1950 with the Divisional bands to form the Royal Marines School of Music at Deal.

The Regimental Marches are justly famous. The Quick March 'A Life on the Ocean Wave', composed by Henry Russell in 1868 with words by Henry Epps Sargent, was first authorised in 1882 and also incorporates a song 'The Sea'. 'Sarie Marais' is the song of the Boer Commandos and was taken into use with the establishment of the Commandos in 1940. The permission of the South African High Commissioner in London was given for it to be adopted by the Royal Marines Commandos in 1952.

A Drummer in a Royal Marines band of 1826. (From the print reproduced in *Britain's Sea Soldiers*).

The Bandmaster, Chatham Division, R.M., in 1851. (From the cartoon by W.G.R. Masters, R.M. Museum).

The Regimental Slow March is 'The Preobrajensky March', presented to the corps by The Earl Mountbatten of Burma in 1964. He recalled that his uncle, the Grand Duke Serge Alexandrovitch of Russia, was one of the last colonels of the Preobrajensky Guards, the senior regiment of the old Imperial Russian Footguards. It was presented on the Tercentenary of the Royal Marines by Lord Mountbatten through H.R.H. Prince Philip, Duke of Edinburgh, their Captain-General. Lord Mountbatten himself was appointed Life Colonel-Commandant of the Royal Marines on 6th August, 1965, being inducted at Eastney that October.

The Inspection piece is an arrangement of the traditional air 'Early One Morning' by Lieutenant-Colonel Sir Vivian Dunn, K.C.V.O., O.B.E., F.R.A.M., R.M.

Two of the Royal Marines Bands have special emblems. The band of CINCNAVHOME, previously the Portsmouth Group band, wear as a cap badge a 'Bursting Grenade and Laurel Wreath', originally granted to the Royal Marine Artillery Band aboard the Royal Yacht by King Edward

An R.M.L.I. band on the march, circa 1900. (From the print by R. Simkin, R.M. Museum).

VII. The 'Cypher of King George V', worn in silver on the grenade, was awarded by that monarch to the same band after his visit to India in 1911. The 'Combined Cyphers of H.M. The Queen and H.R.H. The Duke of Edinburgh', worn in silver above the bursting grenade were awarded to the Portsmouth Group band after the 1954 Commonwealth Tour. All the cyphers are also worn on the white helmet plate. The band of Commando Forces has the 'Prince of Wales Plume' which is worn between the Globe and Laurel and the Lion and Crown and was awarded for the attendance of the Plymouth Divisional band upon H.R.H. on his visit to Canada and Australia in 1921.

It is as well to remember, when watching the glittering spectacle of a Royal Marines Band in immaculate formation, that during World War II some sixty-three of these bands served afloat and, serving as they did in dangerous positions below the waterline mainly manning fire control instruments, their losses were far higher than the ten percent average of the Corps as a whole.

The Junior Band of the Royal Marines School of Music marching through Admiralty Arch. (Royal Marines Official).

Overleaf:
The Patriotic Fund Sword presented to Lieutenant
Robert Hayes, R.M., of H.M.S. *Hydra* for the attack on
Begu in 1807. (R.M. Museum).

Weapons

The Corps has handled a great variety of weapons, and more especially guns, since its inception. From the commando knife to the control of the great 16-inch triple gun turrets of the battleships *Nelson* and *Rodney*, the Marines have learned to master every type of weapon. There can obviously be no complete list of every weapon used by the Corps in over three hundred years of history but a brief mention of a few throughout this period will show their versatility.

At the time of the Corps' foundation in 1664 the men of the Admiral's Regiment were armed with firelocks, then the latest type of small arms weapon. A hundred years later, in 1762, they were using a shortened version of the famous 'Brown Bess', which had originally been introduced in 1731. The barrel was 42 inches in length with a bore of about ¾-inch. Flintlocks were last issued as muskets to the Corps after the passage of almost another century for, in 1839, such muskets were converted by the

A Royal Marines sniper in concealment. The Royal Marines now train all military snipers. (Royal Marines Official).

introduction of a percussion lock. This gave a much improved rate of fire, the ratio of misfires being reduced from 1 in 6½ with the flintlock to 1 in 166. The weapon could also be used in the wet.

Further improvements followed quickly during the latter part of the 19th and early years of the 20th centuries. The 'Minie' rifle of 1851 was a muzzle-loading weapon sighted up to 1,000 yards and its replacement, the Enfield E, was of the same type. At sea, the introduction of the quick firing weapons quickly outdated the rifle and these weapons developed up to the Great War with machine-guns and the heavier pom-poms as well as the Short Lee Enfield. Heavy naval ordance changed out of all recognition as we have noted already but the Marines kept pace.

During the Second World War the emphasis on the light automatic weapon featured in all Commando activity with the American Thompson sub-machine gun giving way to the light, collapsible Sten-gun and subsequent similar types. Post-war has seen the standard Lee-Enfield rifle finally give way to the S.L.R. and during the Borneo confrontation the

A general purpose machine-gun in the Far East. (Royal Marines Official).

Armalite AR 15 was introduced which featured a light alloy receiver, glass fibre body and other advances and was hailed as a 'super weapon'. Today the Marines handle the new sophisticated gadgetry like the 'Bat' tank killer.

Dress and Bases Today

Over the years, the dress and costume of the Royal Marines has altered through an enormous range of uniforms, as a quick reference to the illustrations in these pages will show. Perhaps the most stable element in this historic survey of the Corps would seem to be the bases from which it has operated but even they have changed. The brief existence of the Court Division at Woolwich would appear to have been the biggest alteration during the time of the Grand Divisions and up to the 1920's but since then the many changes that have taken place in bases and barracks are best summarised by listing their present-day functions and locations.

But first we will show the modern forms of dress of the Corps. Our first illustration shows a young officer in the blue ceremonial uniform of the Royal Marines. This uniform can be worn with either the white helmet or the cap as shown here. Officers wear the Sam Browne belt and the open-neck collar, while senior N.C.O.'s wear the Infantry-red sash with the blue or the lovat uniform. A General in the Royal Marines in addition to the normal Royal Marines uniform wears the same uniform as his Army equivalent but always with a white-top cap. Full colonels also wear the same cap badge as Army Colonels and the red patches on the collar but never a high-neck tunic. Field officers' caps are embroidered with distinctive gold oak leaves. The scarlet Mess-uniforms are worn by Officers, Warrant Officers and senior N.C.O.'s as shown in our second illustration.

Our third illustration shows a Royal Marines Director of Music wearing full dress. As can be seen, it features the high-collar and white helmet so typical of the public image of the Corps and in fact, except for the broad red stripe down the trousers and other slight amendments, the bands wear almost the complete pre-war ceremonial dress which was not re-adopted post-war by the rest of the Corps.

The fourth illustration shows a group of young Marines wearing the smart new lovat normal day-dress uniforms which were introduced in 1964. These replaced the khaki battledress and are distinctive. Either the green beret or the red and white cap as shown can be worn with the lovat uniform but band ranks only wear the latter. New recruits wear a blue beret with a red patch and of course have to qualify to wear the proud green beret of the Commando forces.

K

Officer's Uniform, 1974. 'Blues'. (Royal Marines Official).

Showing Royal Marines Mess Dress worn at a dinner in the old Mess Room, Officers Mess, Eastney Barracks. (Royal Marines Official).

The introduction of the lovat uniform was a much-needed and long delayed reform which gave the Corps the smartness and pride of dress that had seemed lacking in khaki but even this move has rather been overtaken by events, for now the more normal day-dress is the green pullover, with reinforced patches, which enables general duties to be carried out with the minimum of interference from clothing.

The white pith helmets of the Royal Marines have now become almost their own traditional form of headdress although they were once only of the same general issue pattern for tropical use as those of the other services.

The ceremonial sword of today is of the infantry pattern of 1895. The grip is of blackened sharkskin and has the royal cypher embodied in the scroll work, while the guard has a fall down on the inside edge to prevent chafing the uniform. The blade is embossed with the Corps insignia and the sword is carried in a leather scabbard.

A Director of Music in Ceremonial Dress.
(Royal Marines Official).

Commando Units wear their own distinguishing lanyards of the Unit Colour. All ranks wear these lanyards on their right shoulder in lovat uniform and their colour identification is as follows: 40 Commando, light blue; 41 Commando, yellow; 42 Commando, white; 45 Commando, red; H.Q. 3rd Commando Brigade, green. H.Q. Commando Forces and the Commando Logistic Regiment wear blue.

Today the Royal Marines have eight main base locations although of course they are seeing service all over the world in detachments large and small. In 1974 Royal Marines were serving afloat and also in Australia, Belgium with NATO, Brunei, the Falkland Islands, Northern Ireland, Iran, Italy, Oman, Singapore, the United States and the West Indies. Since the decision to concentrate the bulk of our forces in the NATO zone the Royal Marines bases have been, in the main, confined to the United Kingdom, and to the south coast in particular.

In London is located, in Whitehall, the Commandant-General's Department, part of the M.O.D. Navy complex. This office is the headquarters

Royal Marines alongside H.M.S. *Victory* wearing the new 'Lovats'. (Royal Marines Official).

180

of the Royal Marines with regard to operations and policy making.

Along the south coast of England, starting in the east and working westward, the first establishment is Deal. Here is the Royal Marines School of Music and here too is located the Physical Training Instruction Wing. Deal was always associated with new entry into the Corps and today it is still 'The Depot, Royal Marines' and here the recruits and junior Marines still carry out their preliminary induction training. H.M. Queen Elizabeth the Queen Mother opened the New Block in 1956.

At Portsmouth, located in the vast Eastney Barracks overlooking the historic waters of Spithead, is the headquarters of the Training Group which commands the training establishments at Deal, Poole and Lympstone. Also at Eastney are located the Royal Marines Museum and Archives, also offices of the Corps official journal, the *Globe & Laurel*. Published bi-monthly, with a circulation which is the envy of many other service magazines, it reflects the continuing affection felt for the Corps by both past and present members.

Poole, in Dorset, houses the Technical Training, Landing Craft and S.B.S. companies. Here are trained all the tradesmen, drivers, landing craft crews, frogmen and the thousand-and-one experts needed to man and maintain a modern mechanised fighting Corps.

Lympstone, near Exeter, is now the largest of the Royal Marines establishments. This is due to the post-war shift of emphasis to the Commandos. At Lympstone is the Commando Training Centre and this includes the Officers and N.C.O.'s Training Wings. In addition to normal Commando training courses all other highly specialised Commando training is carried out here and includes the Signals Training Wing.

For many years based overseas, H.Q. 3rd Commando Brigade is now located at Stonehouse Barracks, Plymouth, as part of Commando Forces R.M. Here also is the Commando Logistic Regiment which includes ordnance, medical, transport and workshop squadrons. Also in Plymouth is based the Air Squadron, equipped with light helicopters. In the traditional gunners stronghold of the Citadel is based the Commando Light Regiment, Royal Artillery and this R.A. element works in complete harmony under the control of Commando Forces. For those who wonder why the Corps, with its proud traditions of the R.M.A., should not have its own supporting artillery, the answer is that at its present strength they cannot accommodate the further specialised training essential for gunnery in addition to the existing highly skilled and specialised Commando training. Plymouth is also the home of two Commandos with 40 Commando at Seaton Barracks and 42 Commando at Bickleigh Barracks.

The only other major units outside the south-east and south-west areas of England are 45 Commando Group at *Condor* Barracks near Arbroath, and 41 Commando Group, at St. Andrews Barracks, Malta. Both these Commando Groups are so termed because they contain additional elements of the Commando Logistic Regiment and a battery of the Commando Light Regiment. They are on duty to protect the northern and southern flanks of the NATO alliance respectively.

Thus stand ready the Royal Marines of today, a Corps with a proud record of over three hundred years faithful service to the country, and a Corps fully prepared and ready to face the future, a future which will surely only add to their many laurels. H.R.H. The Duke of Edinburgh, their Captain-General, once said that, 'Nothing is impossible for the Royal Marines'. With their glorious history and their unique *esprit-de-corps* it seems certain that, wherever called upon they will justify such confidence, *Per Mare Per Terram.*

The Victoria Cross

Ten Victoria Crosses have been awarded to Royal Marines. This, the highest award which may be given for gallantry in the face of the enemy, was founded by Queen Victoria in 1856. It can only be awarded to members of the Services and since the foundation of the award fewer than 1,400 have been awarded. The crosses are still hand cast from the metal of guns captured at Sebastopol during the Crimea War. The ribbon was originally blue for the Royal Navy and Royal Marines and red for the Army but in 1920 this was changed to crimson for all Services.

Following are the official citations from the 'London Gazette'. All ten Crosses are now on display at the Royal Marines Museum.

JOHN PRETTYJOHNS
Corporal, R.M. (2nd November, 1854).
'Reported for gallantry at the Battle of Inkerman, having placed himself in an advanced position; and noticed, as having himself shot four Russians.'

THOMAS WILKINSON
Bombardier, R.M.A. (5th June, 1855).
'Specially recommended for gallant conduct in the advanced Batteries, 7th June, 1855, in placing sand-bags to repair the work under a galling fire; his name having been sent up on the occasion, as worthy of special notice, by the Commanding Officer of the Artillery of the Right Attack.'

GEORGE DARE DOWELL

Lieutenant, R.M.A. (13th July, 1855).

'An explosion having occurred in one of the rocket-boats of the *Arrogant*, during the attack on some forts near Viborg, Lieutenant Dowell (who was on board the *Ruby* gunboat, while his own boat was receiving a supply of rockets) was the first to jump into the quarter-boat of the *Ruby*, and with three volunteers, himself pulling the stroke oar, proceed instantly, under a heavy fire of grape and musketry, to the assistance of the cutter's crew. The Russians endeavoured to prevent his object of saving the men and boat, but Lieutenant Dowell succeeded in taking up three of the boat's crew and placing them on board the *Ruby*; and, on his returning to the spot, was mainly instrumental in keeping afloat, and bringing off the sinking cutter.'

LEWIS STRATFORD TOLLEMACHE HALLIDAY

Captain, R.M.L.I. (24th June, 1900).

'On the 24th June, 1900, the enemy, consisting of Boxers and Imperial troops, made a fierce attack on the west wall of the British Legation, setting fire to the West Gate of the South Stable Quarters and taking cover in the buildings which adjoined the wall.

The fire, which spread to part of the stables, and through which and the smoke a galling fire was kept up by the Imperial troops, was with difficulty extinguished, and as the presence of the enemy in the adjoining buildings was a grave danger to the Legation, a sortie was organised to drive them out. A hole was made in the Legation wall and Captain Halliday, in command of twenty Marines, led the way into the buildings and almost immediately engaged a party of the enemy.

Before he could use his revolver, however, he was shot through the left shoulder, at point blank range, the bullet fracturing the shoulder and carrying away part of the lung. Notwithstanding the extremely severe nature of his wound, Captain Halliday killed three of his assailants, and telling his men 'to carry on and not mind him', walked back unaided to the hospital, refusing escort and aid so as not to diminish the number of men engaged in the sortie.'

WALTER RICHARD PARKER

Lance-Corporal, R.M.L.I. (1st May, 1915).
'On the night of 30th April/1st May, 1915, a message asking for ammunition, water and medical stores was received from an isolated fire trench at Gaba Tepe.

A party of non-commissioned officers and men were detailed to carry water and ammunition, and, in response to a call for a volunteer from among the stretcher bearers, Parker at once came forward; he had during the previous three days displayed conspicuous bravery and energy under fire whilst in charge of the Battalion stretcher bearers.

Several men had already been killed in a previous attempt to bring assistance to the men holding the fire trench. To reach this trench it was necessary to traverse an area at least four hundred yards wide, which was completely exposed and swept by rifle fire. It was already daylight when the party emerged from shelter and at once one of the men was wounded: Parker organised a stretcher party and then going on alone succeeded in reaching the fire trench, all the water and ammunition carriers being either killed or wounded.

After his arrival he rendered assistance to the wounded in the trench, displaying extreme courage and remaining cool and collected in very trying circumstances. The trench had finally to be evacuated and Parker helped to remove and attend the wounded, although he himself was seriously wounded during this operation.'

FRANCIS JOHN WILLIAM HARVEY
Major, R.M.L.I. (31st May, 1916).
'Whilst mortally wounded and almost the only survivor after the explosion of an enemy shell in 'Q' gunhouse, with great presence of mind and devotion to duty ordered the magazine to be flooded, thereby saving the ship. He died shortly afterwards.'

FREDERICK WILLIAM LUMSDEN, D.S.O.
Major, R.M.A.(April, 1917).
'Six enemy field guns having been captured, it was necessary to leave

Lance-Corporal Walter Richard Parker, V.C., R.M.L.I. (From the painting by G.H. Downing, R.M. Museum).

185

them in dug-in positions, 300 yards in advance of the position held by our troops. The enemy kept the captured guns under heavy fire.

Major Lumsden undertook the duty of bringing the guns into our lines.

In order to effect this, he personally led four artillery teams and a party of infantry through the hostile barrage. As one of these teams sustained casualties, he left the remaining teams in a covered position, and, through very heavy rifle fire, machine gun and shrapnel fire, led the infantry to the guns. By force of example and inspiring energy he succeeded in sending back two teams with guns, going through the barrage with the teams of the third gun. He then returned to the guns to await further teams, and these he succeeded in attaching to two of three remaining guns, despite rifle fire, which had become intense at short range, and removed the guns to safety.

By this time the enemy, in considerable strength, had driven through the infantry covering points, and blown up the breach of the remaining gun. Major Lumsden then returned, drove off the enemy, attached the gun to a team and got it away.'

EDWARD BAMFORD, D.S.O.

Captain, R.M.L.I. (7th April, 1918).

'This officer landed on the mole from *Vindictive* with numbers 5, 7 and 8 Platoons of the Marine storming force, in the face of great difficulties. When on the mole and under heavy fire, he displayed the greatest initiative in the command of his company, and by his total disregard for danger showed a magnificent example to his men. He first established a strong point on the right of the disembarkation and, when satisfied that that was safe, led an assault on a battery to the left with the utmost coolness and valour.

Captain Bamford was selected by the officers of the R.M.A. and R.M.L.I. detachments to receive the Victoria Cross under Rule 13 of the Royal Warrant dated 29th January, 1856.'

NORMAN AUGUSTUS FINCH

Sergeant, R.M.A. (7th April, 1918).

'Sergeant Finch was second-in-command of the pompoms and Lewis guns in the foretop of *Vindictive*, under Lieutenant Charles N.B. Rigby, R.M.A. At one period the *Vindictive* was being hit every few seconds, chiefly in the upper works, from which splinters caused many casualties. It was difficult to locate the guns which were doing the most damage, but Lieutenant Rigby, Sergeant Finch and the Marines in the foretop kept up a continuous fire with pompoms and Lewis guns, changing rapidly from

Captain Edward Bamford, V.C., D.S.O., R.M.L.I. (From the painting by W.J. Rowden, R.M. Museum).

Sergeant Norman Augustus Finch, V.C., R.M.A. (From the painting by G.H. Downing, R.M. Museum).

one target to another, and thus keeping the enemy's fire down to some considerable extent.

Unfortunately two heavy shells made direct hits on the foretop which was completely exposed to enemy concentration of fire. All in the top were killed or disabled except Sergeant Finch, who was, however, severely wounded; nevertheless he showed consummate bravery, remaining in his battered and exposed position. He once more got a Lewis gun into action, and kept up a continuous fire, harassing the enemy on the mole, until the foretop received another direct hit, the remainder of the armament being then completely put out of action. Before the top was destroyed Sergeant Finch had done invaluable work, and by his bravery undoubtedly saved many lives.'

THOMAS PECK HUNTER
Corporal, R.M. (2nd April, 1945).
'In Italy during the advance by the Commando to its final objective Corporal Hunter of 'C' Troop was in charge of a Bren group of the leading sub-section of the Commando. Having advanced to within 400 yards of the canal, he observed the enemy were holding a group of houses south of the canal. Realising that his Troop behind him were in the open, as the country there was completely devoid of cover, and that the enemy would cause heavy casualties as soon as they opened fire, Corporal Hunter seized the Bren gun and charged alone across 200 yards of open ground. Three Spandaus from the houses, and at least six from the north bank of the canal, opened fire and at the same time the enemy mortars started to fire at the Troop.

Corporal Hunter attracted most of the fire, and so determined was his charge and his firing from the hip that the enemy in the houses became demoralised. Showing complete disregard for the intense enemy fire, he ran through the houses, changing magazines as he ran, and alone cleared the houses. Six Germans surrendered to him and the remainder fled across a footbridge on to the north bank of the canal.

The Troop dashing up behind Corporal Hunter now became the target for all the Spandaus on the north of the canal. Again, offering himself as a target, he lay in full view of the enemy on a heap of rubble and fired at the concrete pillboxes on the other side. He again drew most of the fire, but by now the greater part of the Troop had made for the safety of the houses. During this period he shouted encouragement to the remainder, and called only for more Bren magazines with which he could engage the Spandaus. Firing with great accuracy up to the last, Corporal Hunter was finally hit in the head by a burst of Spandau fire and killed instantly.

There can be no doubt that Corporal Hunter offered himself as a target

Corporal Thomas Peck Hunter, V.C., R.M. (From the painting by an unknown artist, R.M. Museum).

in order to save his Troop, and only the speed of his movement prevented him being hit earlier. The skill and accuracy with which he used his Bren gun is proved by the way he demoralised the enemy, and later did definitely silence many of the Spandaus firing on his Troop as they crossed open ground, so much so that under his covering fire elements of the Troop made their final objective before he was killed.

Throughout the operation his magnificent courage, leadership and cheerfulness had been an inspiration to his comrades.'

Bibliography

Historical Review of the Royal Marine Corps, by Captain Alexander Gillespie, Royal Marines. Published by M. Swinney, Birmingham, 1803.

Historical Record of the Marine Corps, by R. Cannon. Published 1830.

Historical Record of the Royal Marine Forces. Vols. 1 & 2., by Lieutenant P. H. Nicholas, Royal Marines. Published by Thomas & William Boone, London, 1845.

Historical Records of the Royal Marines, Vol. 1., by Major L. Edye, R.M.L.I. Published by Harrison & Sons, London, 1893.

Story of the Royal Marines — Lectures for Recruits., by Colonel Markham Rose, D.S.O. 6th Edition published 1932.

Britain's Sea Soldiers, Vols. 1 & 2., by Colonel C. Field, R.M.L.I. Published by The Lyceum Press, Liverpool, 1924.

Britain's Sea Soldiers, 1914-1919, by General Sir H.E. Blumberg, K.C.B. Published by Swift & Co., Devonport, 1927.

Random Records of the Royal Marines. Compiled by General Sir H.E. Blumberg, K.C.B. and Colonel C. Field. Published by the *Globe and Laurel*, 1935.

Short History of the Royal Marines, by Colonel G. Grover. Published by Gale & Polden, Aldershot, 1959.

Royal Marines Tercentenary 1664 to 1964, by A. Cecil Hampshire. Published 1964.

Royal Marines Tercentenary 1664 to 1964. Official Account. Printed by W.S. Cowell Ltd., Ipswich, 1964.

Royal Marine Artillery, Vols. 1 & 2, by E. Fraser and L.G. Carr-Laughton. Published by R.U.S.I., London, 1930.

Royal Marines — The Admiralty Record of their Achievements, 1939-45. Official History, H.M.S.O., London, 1944.

The Marines were there, by Sir Robert Bruce Lockhart. Published by Putnam, London, 1950.

Fighting Marines, by Patrick Pringle. Published by Evans Brothers, London, 1966. (Written for children).

The Royal Marines, by Major General J.L. Moulton, C.B., D.S.O., O.B.E., R.M. Published by Leo Cooper, 1972.

Fuel of the Fire, (41 Royal Marines Commando). Published, 1950.

A History of 41 Commando Royal Marines, Unit History.

A History of 43 Commando Royal Marines, Unit History, published 1962.

History of 45 Commando Royal Marines, Unit History, published 1970.

Commando Men, by Lieutenant Bryan Samain, R.M. Published by Stevens & Sons, Ltd., London, 1948.

The Story of 46 Commando Royal Marines, by Captain P.K.W. Johnson, R.M. Published by Gale & Polden, Aldershot, 1946.

48 Royal Marine Commando — The Story 1944-1946. Anon. Privately published 1946.

Haste to Battle, by Major General J.L. Moulton C.B., D.S.O., O.B.E., R.M. Published by Cassell & Co., London, 1963.

Lower the Ramps — A story of 43 Royal Marines Commando, by E.G. Stokes. Published by Brown, Watson Ltd., London, 1955.

A Short History of the Royal Marines in Deal, by Major A.D.H. Jones, R.M. Published 1963.

Green Beret, Red Star, by Major Anthony Crockett, R.M. Published by Eyre and Spottiswoode, London, 1954.

Cockleshell Heroes, by C. E. Lucas Phillips. Published by Heinemann Ltd., London, 1956.

Memoirs of the late Major General Andrew Burn. Published 1816.

Memoirs of Major Oldfield. Published by G.A. Pocock, Dartford.

Memoir of Major Thomas Oldfield, Royal Marines, by Rev. Doctor Mee. Published 1905.

Marine Officer, Vols. 1 & 2, by Sir Robert Steele. Published by H. Colburn, London, 1840.

Memoirs and Services of Lieutenant-General Sir S.B. Ellis. Edited by Lady Ellis. Published by Saunders, Otley & Co., London, 1866.

Per Mare Per Terram, by Major W.H. Poyntz, R.M. Published by the Economic Printing & Publishing Company, London, 1892.

Royal Marines Pocket Book (Four Parts), by Major P.B.H. Wall and Lieutenant G.A.M. Ritson. Published by Gale & Polden, Aldershot, 1945.

Forty Five. The Story of 45 Commando Royal Marines, 1943-1971, by David Young. Published by Leo Cooper Ltd, London, 1972.